Silence

A Spiritual Journey
Through PTSD

Andrew Pearce

SILENCE: A SPIRITUAL JOURNEY THROUGH PTSD

© 2023 Andrew Pearce. All rights reserved. No part of this book may be copied, reproduced or transmitted by any means without prior permission of the author, except in the case of brief quotations embodied in review articles.

Cataloguing-in-Publication entry is available from the National Library of Australia http:/catalogue.nla.gov.au/.

This edition first published in Hackham, South Australia by Immortalise via Ingram Spark in September 2023
www.immortalise.com.au

ISBN paperback   978-0-6457720-6-7
      ebook   978-0-6457720-7-4

Typesetting and cover by Ben Morton
Cover Photo by Andrew Pearce

"Silence"
Copyright © 2002 Pogostick Music (BMI) Pogostick Music (BMI) Pogostick Music (BMI) Bridge Building Music (BMI) Pogostick Music (BMI) (adm. at CapitolCMGPublishing.com) All rights reserved. Used by permission.

"THE ANGEL THAT TROUBLED THE WATERS" by Thornton Wilder Copyright ©1928 by The Wilder Family LLC
From The Collected Short Plays of Thornton Wilder, Volume II. Edited by Tappan Wilder. Copyright 1998 by A. Tappan Wilder, Catharine K. Wilder and Catharine W. Guiles.
Published by Theatre Communications Group, Inc. Reprinted by arrangement with The Wilder Family LLC and The Barbara Hogenson Agency Inc. All rights reserved.

Prologue

A skipping rope…

I found one in my daughter's room the other day among some clothes that I had picked up to wash. It caught me by surprise. I had been doing so well with regards to triggers but this one was so unexpected that I was not on-guard and was left wide open for the unforeseen onslaught.

Sure enough, the mere sight of the skipping rope turned legs that I had thought were so much sturdier to jelly, sent the shakes coursing through my body once again, triggered the thickening of the seemingly ever-present black cloud above my head, and sent all of the promising progress of the previous weeks and months down the drain. I carefully put the offending trigger back down along with the clothes, left the room, closed the door, grabbed Maggie my dog and trusted therapy tool, and went to lie down on my bed.

As Maggie and I lay there, she modelled for me the most useful thing that I could do – sleep. For me, however, a myriad of thoughts crashed through the door, disturbing my rest. Once again, I had no defence against them, a tsunami of pictures and emotions that seemingly swept away all the positive work of the previous few months.

Teaching – even considering the thought of going back, brought the low thundering cloud of dread back onto my horizon.

The playground – the slippery dip, the soccer goals, the cricket net. I found it so hard to give such things even a cursory glance these days.

School desks – all I could see in my head was Azim, in a fit of rage, throwing his desk open, pulling his books out one at a time and ripping them to pieces; with each rip of a page venting all of his frustration: from his years of living in fear for his life back in Sudan, to the relative pettiness of the requests of his teacher.

Azim – that jet black face, so full of anger and hurt and disappointment and fear and trauma and goodness knows what else.

And a skipping rope. I saw it again, placed in desperation around a neck and then a meeting of his eyes with mine in an extended frozen moment…

I still found it inconceivable, even after all of this time, that one object could trigger so many memories. And there were triggers all around me: snipers hidden away in every nook or cranny, behind any bush, lying in wait, patient, disciplined; focused entirely on taking out the target. Feeling utterly exposed, I cautiously picked my way through each day, on edge, knowing that at any moment I could feel the sting of the bullet. Some days it didn't come. On other days, I took several hits. It was never a fatal wound though. Just enough to leave me wounded and bleeding for a day or two, crawling through the jungle, recovering… Until the next time.

If I had known that all this time later I would still be struggling with the memories and the emotions of the incident, would I have intervened? Who knows? It was not a conversation that I wanted to have with myself, I suppose because I feared the reply.

And so, I lived in a twilight zone. Looking back to the past brought on depression and other unwelcome PTSD extended family and friends, as the events replayed themselves over and over again. Looking forward led to anxiety, as I wrestled with the fears that my working life was over and I would never again be useful to anyone. I knew it was better to live in the now: that's what all the professionals were telling me. But the now for me included fatigue, vertigo, nausea, insomnia, substantial weight gain, and days and weeks and months when all I could do was spend the day lying on my bed, hugging my dog.

Prologue

Seriously, apart from hugging my dog, who would want to live that way?

Good/Bad Silence

There are two types of silence.

Or maybe not.

You see, I'm not quite so sure anymore about black and white thinking. Before all that I'm about to tell you happened, I always believed that there was what was "good" and what was "bad." I thought, for example, that there was what seems to be "good" silence and what seems (at the time) to be "bad" silence.

The good silence of a walk along a deserted South Australian beach, with no traffic noise, no TV or phones or devices to distract you. There is wind and there are waves but the silence drowns even their sound out. The good silence of night time, when you know that everyone in the family is home and safe in their beds and they are all recharging from the busyness of the day and dreaming dreams that you couldn't possibly imagine. The good silence of a sleeping, faithful, furry friend, who, without judgement and with complete acceptance, has been with you on every step of your recent journey and now lies sprawled somehow across every square centimetre of your king sized bed, even though she is oh, so very small. The good silence between two people who have been together for decades now and know that they don't always have to say anything, for everything to be said.

Then there is what seems to be the bad silence. The bad silence of waiting for a phone call with what you think will be bad news but the phone remains still. The bad silence of midnight, when your now independent child is out and you cannot hear any hint of the familiar sound of their car. The bad silence between a teenager and a parent, when you know that something is up, that something is wrong between the two of you but you just don't know which words will work and so nothing is said. That awkward silence between people who have just met each other and have covered all the usual topics and now there is nothing. That bad silence that hangs like an awkward adolescent in space when someone asks you how you are and you tell them honestly and then they don't know what to say in reply.

I've experienced both types of silences. And in experiencing both, I can say confidently that I'm not sure anymore how to define either. Good and bad are not as black and white as they used to be. Black and white fade to grey.

But I remember what seemed to be one good silence in particular. I remember lying there, in the dark, breathing in its deliciousness. I remember thinking, "This is what I need. This is what I've been searching for. I've come home." For in that good silence, I sensed peace and rest. In that good silence, I felt safe and secure. In that good silence, I thought I had found all the answers to questions that I had been searching for, for a lifetime.

I remember the good silence of that first night so clearly. I can almost breathe it in again right now. And if I block my ears and listen, I can still hear all that encompassed that good silence.

Sally and I had been planning a move to the South Coast of South Australia for a couple of years. We wanted to move down for a number of reasons, almost all of them to do with our kids. Space for two of them, horse riding for another. Safety also came into it. Our northern suburbs location in Adelaide no longer felt safe since the police station had closed. We'd had cars and letterboxes stolen, fences and house walls graffitied and, once in the dead of night, a man had been chased into our backyard, bashed with a paver on our back doorstep and left there to die. After that, we couldn't wait to get out of there. Our house was only partially renovated and so in the year before the move, there was a flurry of activity, finishing off a house that we would never really enjoy, open inspections and frequent trips down to the South Coast to look for land. We had eventually found two and half acres on an island close to a small country town, made the scary step of buying it before our house had sold, and had given notice at our respective schools.

Looking back now, it was a "bold" move. I had three days of work per week guaranteed down south for the following year but Sally had not found any employment. We felt confident of her securing work however, and even though a week before we were to move we had no house to move to, we were excited. Six days before the move, I managed to score the only rental left on the South Coast, and so it came to pass that a week before Christmas 2008, we loaded the moving vans, grabbed the cat and the dog and drove the hour and a half to what would become our new home town.

That night, the two of us just lay there in the silence, drinking it in; a welcome pool in which to float on our backs. It was one of the best moments of my life.

It had been such a flurry of activity, that that night, as Sally and I lay there in the dark, listening to that sound of silence, we both exhaled a year of frenzied activity, as well as a decade of laying in that very same bed at night listening to buses and cars and sirens, and arguments from next door neighbours, and the all too frequent sound of our letter box being ripped from the ground and dragged down the street, and police cars, and car chases, and men being chased into our backyard and left to die.

That night though, maybe for the first time ever, I listened to silence. I bathed in it. Silence was a soothing balm. Silence produced peace. Silence was good. Silence was very good. I never wanted to be without this silence because in the silence, I found so much rest for my soul. Why would I ever want to be without it?

But there was a silence coming a few years later which would scream disturbing questions, and the answers to those questions, though I searched the silence for a long time – years – set, neat answers to the screaming questions seemingly couldn't be found. It was the "bad" silence.

But even in that bad silence, I found something good.

That Day Pt. 1

There was another silence that I revelled in on the South Coast – the silence of the early morning in the country. Driving to a school at 7am was an unanticipated pleasure, so far removed from the always hectic but snail-like traffic of a metropolitan Adelaide morning.

THAT morning, I was up with the alarm at 6 and on the road by 7. An advantage of leaving this early was that when travelling the Mount Compass Rd there was less chance of becoming caught up in the traffic jam of cows crossing the road either on the way to, or the way back from, their morning milking. When I did get caught by them it didn't bother me too much (apart from the smell). I found it quite quaint and a wonderful reminder of from where we had come. Para Hills West: dirty, smelly, part industrial, and, in the last year or so of our time there, seemingly the crime suburb of Adelaide, what with all of the incidents we had experienced. An age ago in another land, it seemed.

So I arrived at school early that morning – around 7:45. Even though I was at that time working "just" as a TRT (temporary relief teacher), I still liked to arrive early. In fact, there was all the more reason to. The world of TRT is a tough one. You rarely know where you are from one day to the next. You can receive a phone call any time between 6:30 and 8:30 on the day you are required, and often the teacher you are replacing hasn't left any work. And the kids… Well, many of them treat the day as a day off. After all, they don't have a "real" teacher. As a TRT, you have to hit the ground running. If you don't have their attention and respect in the first minute, you will battle to get it all day. It's not an enjoyable job to say the least.

This gig, though, held much promise. The school librarian was rather ill, and I had been offered two weeks of work. This was my second day.

The school was still locked though. I was the first one to arrive and because I was not a permanent teacher, I didn't know how to turn the

That Day Pt. 1

alarm off. So I sat in the car and waited for others to arrive. Eventually other teachers did arrive and I headed into the library. I got settled, spent some time journalling, as was my practice, and then had a look at my day.

It was pretty basic. Being in the library, all I really needed to do was read new books to different classes from the cupboard in the office and then let them return books and borrow new ones. I spent some time browsing and to my delight found the novel that the movie *Hugo* had been adapted from. I spent some time exploring it, loving the fusion of graphic and standard novel.

The bell sounded at 8:30, signalling that students could come to the Library to borrow and return. So I was on duty, helping them through this process. As I did this, I chatted with all with whom I came in contact, trying to remember names, even though at that early stage I hadn't had every class in the school yet and after only a few days I knew I wouldn't be able to remember many anyway. We chatted about books and what they liked doing and I did my best to try to remember each one.

I reflected on what a nice job this was and how I was going to really enjoy the days that remained doing the job…

The morning passed quickly. One class after another filed through and it really was an easy job. I love reading and in my classroom teaching I always loved reading to my classes and really exploring literature in depth. However, I was worried about my throat because it was pretty full on, reading to one class after the other and I was starting to feel a tickle.

Not that it was troubling me while I was reading, but I was also having problems with my left hamstring. I love long distance running and I had recently decided to see how much further I could push myself. I had upped my training, trying to run further and faster. I had managed to increase my speed significantly but this had led to some problems behind my knee, which had been diagnosed as hamstring strain.

It hurt!

Later in the day, I would notice it much more…

Silence: A Spiritual Journey Through PTSD

At lunchtime I went to the staff room. As I didn't have a class, I was just about the first to arrive, so I sat at a vacant table. While I waited for my lunch to heat up, I read the paper. The staff room filled and I noted that, as usual, the cliques formed and sat where they were prone to and the relief teachers were left pretty much alone

No-one sat with me so in the end, I moved to a table and sat with a teacher who I knew lived not far from where we live, and a couple of other teachers. I tried to enter into their conversations but again, they weren't terribly social. I was used to it.

Lunch ended.

I checked my timetable and saw that I had a session with another teacher on the other side of the school. It was to be conducted in their computer suite and I had been asked to assist the kids in their web based research. Again, pretty easy. I thought about what I needed to take and I decided that I didn't need anything. I even decided to leave my phone behind. This was very unusual for me. I always took it with me because I often received calls from other schools during the day, offering me more work. I'm sure that answering the phone during the class wasn't looked upon positively but I had no qualms about it. I needed the work!

But I left my phone behind… I remember thinking about whether I should take it or not and, in the end, deciding that it would be better to leave it behind. It would be the last time that I would ever do that.

I made my way over to the classroom, knocked on the door and entered the room. The teacher was instructing her students about the task that they were going to be doing. I can't remember what it was now.

I introduced myself and she then asked her kids to move quietly into the computer suite.

That Day Pt. 1

Isn't it strange how the most significant moments of our lives come out of the seemingly mundane? My life was about to change forever. My mind was about to be imprinted with pictures that would haunt me for years afterwards and I was totally unaware of this. Had I known, I would have braced myself, ready for the blows. But we live our lives mostly oblivious to the danger around us. It is there every day and most of the time, we sail blissfully past it. I was about to become a rag doll in a hurricane.

As I had entered the classroom, my eyes had been immediately drawn to a boy at a desk at the front and centre of the room. Very dark skinned, tall and wiry, he was a striking looking boy.

After the teacher had finished her instructions and indicated to the class to move quietly into the room, it was this boy, Azim, as I was to find out later, who jumped up and ran full speed out of the classroom, pushing other students out of the way as he went.

His teacher glanced at me, frustrated at Azim's actions. "Azim!" she called out with exasperation in her voice.

I had the impression from the expression with which that one word had been delivered that this may have been an ongoing issue. From my few minutes in the room, I gained the impression that Azim held a fair bit of power in the room. He was a striking looking boy, as I mentioned. Tall, wiry, strong and he was sitting front and centre – the most powerful position on stage. It felt like he was the gravitational centre of the room. All in the room couldn't help but be drawn to him.

The teacher headed to the computer suite. "Azim!" she called out, as if for the umpteenth time. "I asked you to move quietly to the computer suite. Come back into the classroom and sit back down please."

A reasonable request…

But Azim didn't think it reasonable. Or fair. Or logical. From his reaction, it was the most unjust decision ever handed down. Azim shot up from his preferred seat in the computer suite, as if he HAD been shot. Arms waving, he started screaming the most colourful language imaginable, describing how unfair it was and how much the school and everyone in it sucked. He moved back into the classroom though, still yelling and screaming. Azim went to his desk, slumped down in to his desk, narrowed his eyes at his teacher and paused.

Silence… The calm before the storm that I was to become the rag doll in…

In drama, there is a technique used to create dramatic tension on stage. It is when the actors in the scene pause for an extended time with full eye contact. Whatever emotion is being portrayed at that moment, whether love, hate, jealousy or excitement, is amplified to a degree greater than if they had merely maintained eye contact for but a moment. For the audience, the atmosphere becomes supercharged with that emotion.

Here, this classroom had transformed into a stage, and Azim and his teacher were having an extended moment of held eye contact. This extended moment was filled with a perfect storm of rage and sorrow and feelings of injustice and even resignation, as Azim and the teacher eyeballed each other. I was an audience member watching the scene, but in a few moments I would be dragged unwillingly onto the stage and into the story.

As the extended moment broke, Azim grabbed one of his exercise books and slowly and deliberately proceeded to rip it into pieces. He tore and tore, all those feelings that he had used for his laser stare now concentrated into each tearing motion, until the book was in tiny pieces. Then he opened his desk up, found another book and did the same to it. With each rip it was as if he was expelling all of the anger he was feeling toward the school, his teacher and whatever else was on his mind.

That Day Pt. 1

His teacher was not impressed of course and told him that she was going to call the office and ask for someone to come and take him. She asked me if I would mind watching him.

I thought nothing of it, so I agreed. Now that I think about that moment with the benefit of perfect hindsight, the more appropriate option would be for me, a second-day on the job staff member to go to the office for assistance, leaving the regular staff member to deal with the developing incident.

But off the teacher went and I stood there outside the classroom with the door closed and my back to Azim so that he wouldn't have an audience. Every now and then I looked in to see what was happening. Azim had made it through all of his books and paper pads, and was pushing nearby chairs and tables over. His mood had not calmed down at all. In fact, he was becoming more and more hysterical.

I watched closely – not Azim's outward behaviour but I tried to look deeper into him. As I watched, it seemed to me that it was a reaction disproportionate to what had happened. It seemed to me at the time that something else was going on here; as if this was the final straw for Azim. It was as if I had stepped into his story, right at the end of this chapter. It was a chapter that contained a twist to his already tumultuous life and would bring in an unexpected and unwelcome complication to mine. I had little clue as to the part I was about to play but mine would be a key role in this drama.

His teacher returned. I was still standing with my back to the door, guarding it, making sure that no student would enter the classroom but not giving Azim any attention. I didn't want to add fuel to the already raging fire. Azim's teacher joined me and we both stood there with our backs to the door, wondering what to do next.

After a while though, it grew quiet in the room. I figured that Azim had run out of books to rip and furniture to overturn and was either taking a break, or hunting for something else to destroy. I glanced into the room and saw that Azim had stood up and was heading towards the outer door. A little voice in my head said, "Follow him."

That Gentle Whisper. I had heard it before at key moments in my life. Following the words of the Gentle Whisper had led me into and out of jobs, to the other end of the country, into marriage. But they are stories for another time and place. Suffice to say, the Gentle Whisper was familiar to me, and I knew that I needed to do what I had been instructed.

So I asked his teacher if she wanted me to. She indicated, "Yes." I just thought this was the right thing to do, that I would just trail him, making sure he was okay, that he didn't leave the property and if he did that he would be safe, or not harm anyone else. I thought nothing of my decision and had no sense of what was about to happen.

I headed through the classroom and out the door, and turned in the direction I had seen Azim taking. He was heading west back towards the admin block and the library. I made sure that I kept my distance, so that he couldn't see me. I rounded the corner of another building – I can't remember which block it was – but there were middle primary classes. Another student, a boy, was walking towards me, and I asked him if he had seen Azim. The boy indicated that he had circled that classroom block, which meant he may have been heading for the oval, or the playground, so I backtracked, heading east to the playground.

There I saw Azim climbing on to the equipment and sitting down at the top of the slide. I passed a group of three staff members on my way over to the playground, seemingly deep in a post-play-time discussion.

I found a seat near the edge of the playground, about twenty metres away, and sat there for a moment, collecting my thoughts. I could still hear Azim. He was making quite a racket, sobbing and screaming. In the back of my mind I remember thinking, "Why haven't these other staff

That Day Pt. 1

members intervened?" They were engrossed in their conversation still, somehow not even aware that Azim was there.

I sat there on the bench for a while not sure what to do. I didn't know whether to walk over to the playground and try to engage Azim, or – as he didn't know me, to just keep my distance. After a while I decided I should just go over and say something quickly, so I went over and said, "Hi Azim. I'm just going to sit over here to make sure that you are okay."

Azim screamed abuse at me, sobbing and swearing, ordering me away. Such a broken, broken boy. I was beginning to suspect that this reaction wasn't just because of what his teacher had asked him to do. This was the final straw for him. This was just the last episode of a series of unfortunate events that had occurred in his life, stemming back goodness knows how long.

I went back and sat on the bench again, with my back to Azim. Every now and then, I turned around to check on him. I am not sure how long this went on for – maybe five minutes.

After a few turn-arounds though, I saw a sight that burned into my brain. Close up, a frozen moment. It was a scene that would replay over and over in my mind, unwelcome, on automatic rewind, for the next two years...

That Day Pt. 2

In drama, there is a technique I use when teaching improvisation and play building. I introduce the idea of a "frozen moment": a group tableaux that depicts an important moment in time. Often when kids are putting a scene together, I ask them to come up with three frozen moments, in order to find a beginning, middle, and end structure. Then I ask them to fill in the blanks with action and dialogue.

My frozen moment though was singular. There was no other. There was no beginning, middle and end. There was only this one moment. Nothing else existed in my universe but the frozen moment that became the total focus of my attention.

I turned and saw Azim, still sobbing uncontrollably, with some sort of rope in his hands. I looked more closely and then, with a feeling of utter horror rising up from my stomach and into my chest – a palpable, skin crawling moment, from my neck right down my back – I realised that he had fashioned this rope into a noose and was lifting it up, preparing to place it around his neck…

At this point, everything to do with Azim came sharply into focus. It was as if my eyes suddenly had a zoom lens, and I was standing only centimetres in front of him, not the twenty metres or so that I was. I was told later that this is a normal phenomenon in stressful situations. The brain brings into focus only that which is vital, and blanks out all else. Concentration is required only for that which requires attention. It's all to do with the "Fight, Flight or Freeze" response. We concentrate on that which is important, decide whether to stay and fight, or flee, or freeze, and then take the decided upon action. My brain decided to stay, horrified though I was. I certainly didn't make a conscious decision to stay or leave. It was if my brain was on auto pilot. My executive functioning took over and it was as if I wasn't there anymore. Certainly the next forty or so minutes felt like that.

That Day Pt. 2

With my telescopic vision, I could see clearly now that it was a skipping rope which perhaps had been left on the play equipment. Such an innocent item, neither good nor bad. Just a piece of rope. But Azim had seized upon it and was fashioning it into a noose, still sobbing and wailing. When I looked into his tear-filled eyes, I sensed that he was determined to see this task through to the end.

"What do I do first?" I thought. "Do I go over to Azim? Or do I go and get help?"

It was here that I felt my first moment of isolation. A moment of silence that terrified me. No answer to my question. No one to come alongside me and support me. It was here that I first set foot onto a lonely beach and started my run.

The staff members about fifty metres away remained oblivious to all that was happening. They were still deep in conversation. I remember feeling at the time, even at this early stage, that, apart from Azim, I was alone in this. It was just Azim and me, together, centre stage, shared top status. Even though others would enter and play important roles, we were the two main actors who would see this scene through to the end. It was lonely in that spotlight. I drew in breath and started to improvise.

I decided to go over to Azim. I ran over to him, as fast as my hamstrung leg would allow. With urgency in my voice, I said to Azim not to put the noose around his neck. In my head, it sounded pathetically unconvincing. I felt like there was no power at all in my words. It was one of those recurring nightmares where you are in danger and can't yell loud enough to be rescued.

And this feeling was confirmed as Azim, still sobbing – a lost, broken boy it seemed, slowly and deliberately placed the noose around his neck. To me it was as if this was his final solution; that he had indeed come to the end of his rope, that he had tried everything else and this was it. This was the answer that made the most sense to solve his problem.

At this point I realised that I needed help. I raced over to the group of three adults about fifty metres away. They were still chatting, inexplicably unaware of what was unfolding, though from where they were standing, you could clearly see and hear that something was wrong. I had no time to process that one, and even to this day, I cannot explain it. I quickly explained what was happening though, asked for help and sprinted back to the playground, dodgy hamstring screaming out at me by this stage. I climbed the equipment, reached out to the knot that he had tied around the equipment and untied it as Azim was preparing to lower himself over the edge.

Azim didn't like this at all. He screamed at me to stop and to go away. He came towards me threateningly, as if he was going to push me from the equipment, so I quickly got down. Azim got down too, though I can't remember how.

What followed after this, was a pursuit around the school yard. Two women were helping me now. One was a Deputy Principal and the other was an SSO, on her second last day at the school. We followed Azim to some soccer goals. He wanted to tie himself to the crossbar but I got there before him and so he turned towards the cricket practice nets. He ran around to the back of the nets and in an instant, effortlessly it seemed, scaled the side of the nets, and was scrambling on the top wire covering before I knew it. Jane, the SSO and I glanced at each other, having the same thought.

"Who's going up there?"

I knew I couldn't because of my hamstring. Jane gave it a go but grabbed hold of the wire so tightly that she cut her fingers. Azim scrambled over to the other side of the nets, to the part where there was no side. Nothing between the edge of the nets and the ground. I ran around to get as close as I could to him. He began to tie the skipping rope to the edge rail of the nets.

That Day Pt. 2

It was now that a feeling of dread coursed through my body. I felt it in my heart and in my head. It weighed down on me heavily and my legs turned to jelly. It was the feeling that this might not end the way I wanted it to.

"How am I going to stop this?"

"This is going to end badly".

The feeling of dread was quickly followed by the feeling again that I was alone in this, even though others were now present. I somehow knew that it had to be me who would have to try to save him. The other people seemed to be blinded to what was actually going on. It felt like I was the only one who understood what was unfolding here and the others were playing catch up.

For some reason, I was here at this school, on this day to save Azim.

I didn't know if I could do it…

I looked up at Azim. He was sobbing as he finished tying the rope. He looked at me and again screamed for me to go away. I started talking to him. I said, over and over again with uncertainty in my voice, "I will not let you do this."

Inside, I didn't feel quite so convinced. Inside my doubts were rising. "I don't think I'll be be able to catch him if he jumps." It was a feeling of rising helplessness.

The deputy principal was standing nearby at this stage, just watching. "Do you have a phone?" I asked.

"Yes," she replied.

"Call 000," I said, with as much calmness in my voice as I could muster.

"Do you think so?" she asked.

"Yes, we need to. We need help." I insisted.

I couldn't believe it. Again, it seemed that the others around me were frozen, that they were somehow looking at a different scene to the one that was being played out before me. I couldn't work it out. But there was a certainty in my heart that I knew what to do. There was no time to waste, no time to ask questions or discuss. We had to be decisive and efficient.

The deputy called 000, though I could sense she was doing it with some reservations.

Meanwhile the standoff continued. "I will not let you do this." I kept saying it, over and over again, hoping that Azim would be convinced by my voice and that he would take me at my word. I hoped that the power of my words would either keep him up there or force him to come down safely. The third option, the one that sent dread and adrenaline coursing through my system was the one I feared would happen.

Azim wasn't convinced…

After a time, still sobbing, Azim lowered himself over the edge of the crickets nets. I watched on in horror. Again, it seemed like I was a spectator. It seemed like it wasn't me living this moment but that I was watching it on TV or at the movies. I knew that I couldn't change the station to more pleasant viewing, or excuse myself from the cinema to get popcorn. I couldn't take my eyes from the screen. I had to watch. I had to act.

As Azim's feet came within range, I grabbed at them and held on tight. I don't have the best of fingers. Hyper-extensive finger joints make it difficult for me to grip onto things at the best of times, but I did my best.

That Day Pt. 2

Azim was still sobbing and screaming but I called out to him with desperation in my voice.

"I will not let you go. I will not let you do this. If you fall, I will catch you."

"I will not let you go. I will not let you do this. If you fall, I will catch you."

"I will not let you go. I will not let you do this. If you fall, I will catch you."

I said it over and over, a mantra. A mantra is recited in some religions in an effort to bring about that which is supposedly true. Mantras are seen as being crucial to the maintenance and order of the world. My world at that moment had been thrown into chaos, so I recited my newfound mantra as much to me as to Azim, trying to convince myself that this indeed would be the outcome. And while this was all occurring I held on for dear life to Azim's feet, as he, just as desperately, pushed down as hard as he could, in an effort to make me lose my grip. He began to realise that he needed to change tactics.

There was a lot of debris up on the cricket nets, having found a home up there, I suppose, after kids during playtimes either deliberately or not, threw things up there and then found no way of getting them down. Whilst pushing down with his legs and continuing with his incessant sobbing and screaming, Azim scrabbled around in the debris and came upon a sharp stick. He took hold of it and, with fury in his eyes, leant down and proceeded to stab my hands with it.

I held on as best I could. "I will not let you go. I will not let you do this. If you fall I will catch you."

Over and over and over.

Eventually my hands began to bleed and the pain became almost unbearable. I felt my strength, both in my hands and in my heart, rapidly waning.

Some time during all of this, however, as my body was wrestling with holding on to Azim's feet, my mind was wrestling with alternatives, and it came up with an idea. I had asked Jane to go and get a chair and some scissors from a classroom. They were brought to us by a boy, who watched on, fascinated with the performance.

While still holding on to Azim, I climbed up on to the chair, and with the scissors, cut the skipping rope from the cricket nets. Azim was furious. With the remainder of the skipping rope still around his neck, he screamed even more, if that was possible, jumped up and scrambled around to the other side of the cricket nets.

"Quick, he's going to do it again!" I called to Jane. I grabbed the chair and ran around to where he was tying the rope again. I climbed up on to the chair and cut the rope again, this time trying for some distance between the cricket nets and the point of the cut. My mind began to see how we might foil this suicide attempt.

Of course, Azim scrambled back around to the other side, retied the rope and started again. So again I ran around, climbed up on the chair and cut the rope. This happened perhaps five times.

I was so tired. This incredible feeling of weariness engulfed me. It wasn't a physical one – I could run all day. The weariness was more emotional, a tiredness deep, deep down inside. I remember thinking, "I don't know how much longer I can go on." I just wanted to curl up into a ball and sleep. I didn't want to be doing this any more.

After cutting the rope so many times and attempting to make the cut closer and closer to Azim each time, the rope did indeed become too short for Azim to tie to the nets. He realised this suddenly. And it made him very angry.

That Day Pt. 2

I will never forget the look on his face. It will be one of the images of the day that will be forever burned into my brain. This one expression – of unbridled anger, and another – of a frightened boy on a slippery dip, placing a noose round his neck. Two frozen moments. This look, a mixture of utter sorrow but also hatred. Hatred it seemed, that was directed towards me. He stared at me, eyes burning holes into me.

"Why do you hate me?" I silently questioned him. "I don't understand. I am trying to save your life, Why do you hate me for it?"

As if in reply, Azim picked up a piece of debris from the top of the nets and motioned that he was going to hurl it at me – eyes opening even wider, if that was possible.

I picked up the chair, held it in front of me and backed off. The debris that Azim had picked up was a large piece of asphalt. He hurled it at me, the full force of the sorrow and anger that he had been screaming with for the past half hour, now concentrated into the throw.

He picked up another and hurled it again, this time at another male teacher who had arrived on the scene. Azim's attention was drawn from me, so I again moved closer, chair in front of me. I was afraid that Azim would jump and wanted to be close by. I thought that if he knew that someone was close by, then he wouldn't jump.

This scene played out again and again also. Azim would pick up a piece of asphalt, we would back off, he would throw it at one of us and then we would get close again. It was a pathetically hopeless situation. We had indeed reached a standoff. No one had the advantage. No one would win. Stalemate.

The police eventually arrived to end the standoff. They had a brief discussion with me about the situation. A ladder finally arrived and one of them climbed it. Azim scrambled to the other side of the nets and jumped off, fracturing an ankle. But at least he was safe.

At this point I felt that my part in Azim's story was complete and I withdrew from the situation. I felt there were so many people there by now – two police patrols and an ambulance plus, by now, many, many more staff members, as well as dozens of students who were crowded up to their classroom windows. The school had been locked down I think but that didn't stop many students from witnessing all that had happened.

That my part in his story was complete was true. I only ever saw Azim again once more. What I didn't realise though, was that these events, which likely totalled forty minutes, were about to have an incredibly profound effect on my life. My story was about to encounter a twist which I hadn't anticipated. I guess that's why they call them twists. If you expected them, you would be prepared for the turn in the story. I was completely unprepared.

Aftermath

Numb. I've heard that used as a description for the aftermath of critical incidents and before the moment that I had just experienced, I had always found it hard to fathom. But in the hours afterwards, I truly felt this way. It seems my brain had administered anaesthetic to my system to prevent my body from feeling too much.

The Deputy Principal and I walked off to the admin block. She wanted to get me away from the scene as quickly as possible, for which I was grateful. Although she had been just a bystander, she was visibly shaken. She was openly crying and shaking substantially. For me, my eyes felt stuck open. I just stared ahead. The Deputy was talking a lot but I wasn't really tuned in. I heard her voice but it was in the background, like conversations that you catch snippets of whilst dining out.

I went to the staff room, poured a cup of tea and took it to her office, where we we sat down. I remember that on sitting down, I started to shake. I was cold. It was a warm early Autumn day but I shivered. I know now that I was in shock.

The Deputy kept talking but I only answered to whatever she said in mono syllables. I sipped on my tea, while she rang her partner. She spoke with him for a while, explaining what had happened, crying some more and then hung up. She asked me if I wanted to call Sally. I knew that Sally would be in class and wouldn't be able to come to the phone, so I declined.

We sat and debriefed about the whole incident but I wasn't really there. Once again, I felt like my eyes were glued open at the widest diameter possible and that if they could possibly open any further, they might pop out. I sat there and stared into the distance, vaguely aware of the conversation that apparently I was involved in. It was another out of body experience: I observed myself motionless, apart from hugging a cup of tea tightly with both hands, taking the occasional sip, speaking to another person in single syllables.

The deputy started to write a Critical Incident Report, occasionally asking me to contribute. I just had no interest in the whole thing. The events were sketchy to me at that stage. I think my mind had blanked them out for a time, so that my body could remain functioning. My brain decided to hide the whole incident in a quiet, safe corner, to be brought out at another time when it was a little safer to consider what had happened.

A counsellor was called and she arrived shortly afterwards. We both chatted with her but I really had nothing to say. She listened and gave me a few brochures but I remember feeling that it was a waste of time. She came again the next day and I had to talk to her a second time but again felt it didn't do me any good. I suspect it was because I wasn't ready for it. The problem was, I didn't know this. I wasn't in any state of mind to recognise that I had shut down and I had no one familiar around me to see what was happening and to come alongside me. As a relief teacher, you have no home base. You drift from school to school, with no support with the harder issues of teaching. This was certainly one of those moments. At the end of each TRT day, instead of having a core group of colleagues to debrief with, I just packed up my things and headed home.

I left school early that day. I just wanted to get out of there. I honestly cannot remember what I did once I left. It was all a bit of a blur. I may have driven around for a while. I may have visited the nearby beach I think but I am just not sure. I really have no memory of it. A huge chunk of time lost.

My brain had gone into protection mode already. I drove the forty minutes home in a daze, not thinking about or feeling anything. What had happened was so out of the ordinary. One doesn't go to school in the morning, expecting to save a life. Maths, spelling, sport, or the important things like writing, music and drama. Those are the things that make up a

Aftermath

teacher's day. Not a real life drama. Not holding up a boy so that he does not choke to death. My brain just couldn't reconcile what had happened and so it numbed itself, so that it didn't have to think about it for a time.

Later when everyone else's school day was over I drove to Sally's school to find her. She was having a performance review meeting; that wonderful occasion several times a year, when you come before your line manager to talk about what you have been doing.

I went to the front desk and the principal was there. I asked to see Sally but she told me that I couldn't because she was in the meeting. I explained to the principal what had happened but still she would not let me see her. She could not be interrupted. In the greater scheme of things, a performance review meeting was deemed more important than my state of mind by someone who should have known better.

I couldn't believe it. I had to wait another two hours until Sally arrived home. It was awful.

While I waited I went for a long run to try and clear my head. Running entered my life during my teenage years, and it is something that has been with me ever since. I both love it and hate it. I love and hate the mental struggle mainly. In the main, that's what it is. A battle of the mind.

So, when I arrived home, I went for a run. I think I was still in shock. I remember feeling like what I had been through wasn't real – as if I had been watching someone else's life, or had viewed a report on the evening news about some awful incident at a school a long way away.

But not to me. It hadn't happened to me. My day had been completely normal. I had gone to school that morning, taught some delightful students and gone home.

Yes, that's what had happened. Surely?

After all, you don't go to school expecting that you are going to have to save a life. Do you?

The next few days of school were hard. I felt like I was on the verge of something disturbing the whole time. I kept thinking, "I don't want to be here. I can't do this anymore."

They were feelings foreign to me. I had been a successful teacher for 25 years. I was confident, talented, able to motivate kids and form tight knit communities in my classrooms.. These feelings unnerved me. Most of the days in the aftermath I couldn't get through to the end of the day. Panic would set in, the walls would close in around me, I would have "out of body" experiences, where I would look down and see myself talking to students who had come into the library, tears would well up into my eyes, a dark cloud would gather over my head, or, most frightening of all, images of slippery dips and cricket nets and skipping ropes fashioned into nooses would flash through my mind. My legs would turn to jelly and I would be floored, unable to do anything. All of this was happening in my head while I was actually teaching a class. I was a swan on a tranquil lake. On the glassy surface, serene and graceful, while underneath, webbed feet paddled furiously trying to escape the jaws of whatever it was that was pursuing me.

A week after the incident, I was summoned into a Deputy Principal's office and she asked me to relate the incident to her again because the Education minister had requested a report. It seemed that the incident had created ripples up through the ranks. So, I went through it in great detail again, answering every question and every request for further detail. By the end of it, of course, I was a mess. I tried to go back to work but I just couldn't focus

The last three days at school were like this. I would turn up, bright and early each morning, hoping to be able to do my job. I would do my best with classes that came in, however I found that my resources for coping with bad behaviour, my enthusiasm for literature, and my interest in building the skills of the students who came in, became non-existent.

Aftermath

I was in survival mode. Looking back, I can see that now. Automatically, my brain had taken over control of a number of systems because it recognised unconsciously I wasn't able to see that I was heading towards a dark place. So, it focused all its attention on getting me to school and protecting my system from harm – in the form of misbehaving students, or sounds and vision which threatened to trigger the memories of the incident.

Midway through most of the days, I fell in a heap, emotionally exhausted, nothing left to give. I would then tell the school I needed to go and I would escape as quickly as I could. The school was good about it. They still paid me and that was my main concern.

The incident happened in the second last week of school before the 2012 Easter/first term break. Mercifully, the holidays came and I spent my time in the garden, mowing and weeding. Weeding and mowing. We have a two and half acre block and, at that stage, were not in a position to be able to afford a ride on mower. It was certainly on "the list" but a long way down it. And so, I struggled with our standard lawnmower, pushing through two and half acres of weeds. It kept me in shape for certain and it was a welcome silence from what had occurred. Out on the block, as I mowed, I entered a place where events like boys tying skipping ropes into nooses, scaling cricket nets and hanging themselves don't occur. Out on the block, as I mowed, there was silence in my head and in my heart, as I focused on the next weed.

By the end of the two weeks of holidays spent mainly mowing, I felt like I was over the worst of it.

The Deeper Hurt

For several days after the incident with Azim, my hands hurt terribly as a result of his attack on my hands with rocks from on top of the cricket nets. With numerous deep, deep cuts, there was little I could do apart from ensuring that I kept them clean and free from infection. I knew that eventually they would heal. My hands might bear scars eventually but I knew that the deep wounds would be okay.

Looking at my hands now, eight years later, there is not even a hint of scars. I can examine my hands very slowly and carefully but cannot identify any marks on them that might possibly be a reminder of that day. And though in the first few days and weeks my attention was drawn to the pain in my hands, what I wasn't aware of was another wound deeper inside me that was festering away. The physical symptoms were evident initially in those first few hours after the incident. The shaking, dry mouth, and shivering body. Once they dissipated, however, I failed to notice that, though the outward symptoms and cuts were no longer evident, deep deep down an open wound remained untended. The events of that day has set in motion a domino-like chain that some weeks later would not end well for me.

Just off the New England Highway between Sydney and Brisbane lies Mt. Wingen. This mountain issues a constant smell of acrid sulphur. Mt Wingen is not a volcano however. Instead, a seam of coal below the surface of what is colloquially referred to as "Burning Mountain" has been on fire for what is believed to be about 6000 years. The local Wanaruah people have a Dreaming story which explains how the phenomenon started but it is not known exactly how it began. Some suggest a lightning strike; others propose that it was set in motion by the Indigenous land management practice of burning scrubland in order to encourage revegetation.

The Deeper Hurt

Whatever the cause, the fire still burns underground. It began with a spark. The spark grew and, because it was left to gather strength unseen below the surface, today it rages and cannot be controlled. A phenomenon that cannot be explained.

And deep in my mind a similar spark was left to gather strength unseen. While I spent the holiday period mowing lawns and gardening in an effort to "get away", I didn't notice the spark inside had become a flame, the flame had become a fire, and the fire was developing into an uncontrollable raging inferno. It was unnoticed and unchecked, below the surface, but five weeks later the signs would become clear to everyone.

And that's the thing about PTSD (because, of course, unbeknownst to me, that is what was developing in me) and other mental illnesses. If someone breaks an arm, the arm is put in a sling or plaster in order to support the injury and immobilise it so that it can heal properly. With PTSD, there is certainly something awry but it is not always clear what this is and so supporting the injury and immobilising it so that it can heal properly is extremely difficult.

With an infection, such as a cold or a stomach bug, the effects of the infection can be clearly seen, even if the source of it cannot. If someone has a cold, then it is all they can do not to sneeze or cough. In fact, the cough or the sneeze serves a purpose in clearing the body of the infection. With PTSD however, the effects can be secreted away by the sufferer. One could hide away in their own little world fairly easily, and their closest family or friends may not notice the effects. Many of my friends, not including some that I kept in touch with via social media, had little idea how I was spending my days. I am certain they would have reacted with a good deal of shock if they had discovered that once it was diagnosed, most of my days were spent lying on my bed in a darkened room, unable to do anything much at all, save hug my dog.

PTSD causes a deeper wound than many physical injuries, I believe. In my life, I have had broken arms, fingers, pulled muscles, dislocated kneecaps, a damaged eye and, for a time, these injuries caused me great pain. But I recovered from them without much fuss or hassle and I think it was because the symptoms could be clearly seen and the treatment was obvious. But the wound caused by PTSD is insidious and because it is not so obvious, treatment is often delayed until the wound is so infected that more extreme measures need to be taken. PTSD can become a coal seam fire: a raging, uncontrollable blaze, hidden deep beneath the surface, whose effects can sometimes be sensed, as in a sulphurous odour, but never totally understood.

How can such a fire burn unchecked?

The End

It did burn unchecked though. It was there, bubbling below the surface. Molten rock, searching for a weak spot in the crust to break through and create havoc. I think I was aware of the growing pressure at the time, but I chose to ignore it. I had to work after all. As a TRT, there is no such thing as sick leave. If you don't work, you don't get paid. This added impetus to the impending eruption. It was the weak spot, through which the lava would eventually flow.

At the beginning of Term 2, I had a 2 week block at the local school. It was a tricky class with a couple of boys who displayed major behaviour challenges. They rarely turned up though so that was a bonus. Things seemed to be going smoothly with the class, as they grew used to me and I to them. But then one day, one of the boys – a boy on the autism spectrum did turn up and everything changed. You could see where the power in that class lay.

Something triggered this boy at one stage and so he jumped up and ran out of the classroom. Naturally, I walked to the classroom door to watch where he was going. As I walked to the door, I asked another child to go to the office for help. All very normal really.

As I watched, I saw him go to the playground and climb the play equipment....

My whole body went limp.

I felt the energy drain away.

Legs turned to jelly.

I started shaking.

I broke out into a cold sweat.

Just like that. Out of nowhere. Completely unexpected.

I recovered after a few minutes but the incident unnerved me. I began to worry. I had felt okay during the holidays but after that moment, I could sense something 'gathering' over my head: a darkness in the air.

I worked through those two weeks fairly well. It was good to be working. It was satisfying to be productive. But always, as I was working with the children, there was an awareness from time to time of this feeling over my head – a gathering of a dark, foreboding cloud. An increasing sense of dread.

About a week into this teaching block, there was another incident one morning. The kids were simply coming into the classroom for the beginning of the day. Nothing unusual but all of a sudden I felt like I wanted to run and hide. A panic rose up inside of me and I couldn't think what it was that I had to do. There was an overwhelming feeling that I couldn't remember how to teach, or how to manage a class. All my confidence was lost for a good five minutes.

The school counsellor, a good friend of ours, was walking past as this incident occurred. I told her what was happening and she took me through some breathing. I was okay after a while but again, it unnerved me. I didn't understand what was going on. I continued to be conscious of the growing feeling of dread. I was aware of the signs of depression and I was making sure that I was running, eating well, keeping in touch with friends and continuing to journal, in an effort to stave off that darkness. The panic, the cold sweats and the shaking were new though. I didn't know what to make of them. They were new demons that I had never faced.

I made it through those two weeks of teaching but by the end of it I had become physically sick. I had lost my voice and developed a bad chest

The End

infection and as a consequence, I was sick all of that weekend. I was worried because I had a three week teaching block coming up at the school where the incident with Azim had occurred. I think it had been offered to me out of sympathy really. I had prepared for it thoroughly but ill health, combined with the nervousness of having to go back there, made for an anxious combination.

I had arranged to visit there on the Monday for the full day to observe the class I was to take charge of, and plan. I still went even though I felt really sick and I had no voice at all. I was to be paid for the day, even though it was a planning day for me. So, after I had met with the teacher I was replacing, I sat in the Staff Room, planning my two week programme.

As I was working, the principal came in and had a chat with me. She mentioned that the Education Minister was coming for a tour of the school the following day. I said that at that stage I didn't know if I would be able to do the first day because of my health. I also asked why the minister was coming to the school because it was an unusual occurrence. The principal said it was because they had had a "critical incident" at the school during Term 1. I asked what had happened.

She said that a boy had tried to hang himself on the playground. I casually said that I knew about that. She stopped for a moment. It was obvious that, even though I had spent a good deal of time with her after the incident, she had forgotten who I was. Realisation came over her face as she recognised me. I was a bit taken aback by this. I found it very hard to fathom that she didn't know who I was after all that had happened because she had spoken to me a number of times about it afterwards. Anyway, she asked me how I was going.

I decided to tell her the truth…

I shared with her that I was having some trouble with visions of the event occurring while I was teaching and that they were coming without warning. At the time, I didn't know that they were called "flashbacks" and that they were a symptom of PTSD. I was still not aware about what was happening to me. Of course, I had heard of PTSD but thought the main sufferers were military personnel who had seen combat. Surely, it couldn't be brought on by what I had been through?

The principal listened with a concerned expression on her face. When I had finished sharing, she asked me if I was going to be able to do the three weeks. A fair enough question I guess after all I had shared. I appreciated her concern but I said that I was determined to do it and that I would see how I went. You see, at that stage I was not aware of any options available to me. No one had let me know that I could possibly qualify for workers' compensation. I believed that, as a relief teacher, I had one option; that I would just have to keep working in order to be paid.

The Principal and I had another chat later on in the week, as we walked the class I was taking to a nearby community garden. As we walked, she asked me about my background. I shared with her about my background in Special Ed, our teaching in private schools for most of our lives, and our difficulty finding secure work after our move down to the South Coast.

She said she couldn't understand it when people said that to her, stating work was easy to find if you were a good teacher. She told me to regard the three weeks as a trial period and that if I was proficient enough I would have a good chance of getting contracts there. Talk about extra pressure! Here I was, still rather ill, sharing with her about my concern with flashbacks, and the difficulty in securing work and now, in addition, the pressure of needing to impress the principal, lest I not work there again.

The End

The class that I was taking was a 3/4 all boys class. They were extremely hard; one of the worst behaved classes I had ever come across, and I had had a few in my time. They had terribly low literacy and numeracy levels – critically low and this was one of the factors which led to some extreme behaviours. There were boys attacking each other physically and verbally with great regularity during class time. I devised a behaviour management strategy for them – I have no memory now what it entailed but after the first day it seemed to work quite well.

It was obvious that these boys were not used to being engaged with learning much at all – or working without interfering with each other, or working without yelling and screaming. After a couple of days the student support officers (SSOs) were commenting on how well the boys were working. Despite my feeling really sick still and the ever constant view of the cricket nets, clearly seen from the window, I was pretty happy with their feedback. We seemed to be getting somewhere.

Yes, that's right. You read that casual phrase that I slipped in there correctly. The ever constant view of the cricket nets. The cricket nets were right next to the classroom where I was teaching. Constantly in my view. I wasn't aware of it at the time but as I reflect, I was on edge, on guard, the whole time.

There is a scene in the movie, *A Beautiful Mind* where Russell Crowe's character John Nash has come to terms with the fact that he has schizophrenia and that a number of the people who have befriended him over the years are not real. He has tried medication to deal with it but that leaves him lethargic, unable to display his love for his wife and, with a deadened mind, devoid of its former creativity. After another episode, in a meeting with his psychiatrist he states that he will "apply his mind" to the problem – something that he has been doing with mathematical problems his entire academic life.

And so, for the remainder of the movie, we see John Nash in various situations on the university campus coming across these figments of his imagination – people who were once integral to his life, and having to put them out of his sight. At times we see him holding up his hand in refusal as the characters attempt to converse with him. At times the pressure is unbearable, as they accuse him of betraying their friendship after all of this time.

It was like this for me in a way. The cricket nets were there, in my sight, but unlike John Nash in "A Beautiful Mind", they were not constructs of my mind. They were real. They were there. All the time. But like John Nash, I attempted to "apply my mind" to the problem, by, if not keeping them from my view completely, then at least keeping them at the periphery of my vision. I held my hand out to them, refusing to let them affect me. Yes, that was a good plan.

Not.

On the Thursday, two days into the teaching block, a Deputy Principal arranged for me to meet with Azim. She thought it would be good for both of us. I had yard duties to do during my time there, and she was concerned with what would happen to either of us if we came across each other unexpectedly in the yard. I really appreciated the thought and agreed to meet with Azim, though somewhat nervously.

During the meeting, Azim was quite unresponsive and ignored me almost totally. He made no eye contact with me at all. I didn't know if it was embarrassment, or shame, or more likely perhaps, whether it was a cultural thing. Perhaps Sudanese custom was to avoid eye contact in some situations. I was ignorant to the reasons, but, quite frankly, by then I really didn't care.

It was an incredibly awkward situation but at the time, I was glad that it had been organised. I didn't have any flashbacks, I didn't break out in a cold sweat and there wasn't a panic attack in sight. I began to think that maybe I was on top of this.

The End

The afternoon following the meeting though was really, really hard. The meeting with Azim had brought the event back to my mind all over again, even though I wasn't aware of it and my mind didn't like it – not one little bit. It began to go into protection mode.

In my teaching, I started to have the sensation again of not being able to remember what to do and freezing. These boys were still really hard to manage. I had to be on top of them the whole time, otherwise they would have been all over me. Outwardly, I was in control: calm, confident, patient and the obvious authority in the classroom. Inwardly, I felt like I wanted to curl up in a ball and hide. I felt exposed. I felt that I was going to be ripped to pieces by these boys. There were behaviour incidents constantly and inside, I felt powerless to do anything, even though they were still open to my correction.

To be honest, I had had enough. I felt like sitting back in my chair at the desk and just letting them go for it.

I had the same experience all through the next day, which was Friday but made it through, outwardly unscathed. Inwardly, I felt numb and detached though. I didn't feel as if I had any control and I had lost the desire to teach these boys. Again, this worried me. I had spent twenty five years helping kids, some from dire circumstances. I had always been for the underdog; acting as an advocate, believing in the seeming lost cause when it seemed that no one else would. I always tried to seek out the kids who were really struggling. Always. It was where I shone.

But now, here was a whole class full of lost causes and I felt that I just couldn't do it anymore. I felt like I was the lost cause this time but there was no one, save my wife and kids, believing in me. I planned over the weekend and had everything ready for the week. As it turned out, it was the week when a mandated government testing regime was to occur, and with these boys it was going to be extremely hard. This added to the pressure I was already feeling.

I arrived there on the Monday feeling very, very low. It was dark. So dark. I didn't think it would get darker (I found out a few months down the track that I was wrong about this) and I can't remember much at all about that day. But I got through it. There were many, many behaviour incidents though. One boy in particular was out of control. I suspected that there was an intellectual disability there but it didn't excuse the fact that he was constantly physically attacking other boys and I had to call for the office to have him removed time and again.

At the beginning of the day, the boys were supposed to have a language lesson with another teacher, and this was to be my preparation time. I took the boys over to the room but the teacher wasn't there. We waited and waited but the teacher didn't come. I sent my teacher support person over to find out where she might be, to no avail. The teacher eventually turned up 20 minutes late. There had been some mix up and she didn't know what was going on either. It wasn't her fault but this added to my already grave condition because these boys had nothing to do in the room while we waited. I didn't know any computer logins and so I couldn't get anything up and running for them to work on. It was an unfortunate, bad joke with no punchline to save it.

In the time that was left, I went back to the classroom but I could not focus on any preparation. I was so, so tired. I just put my head down on the desk and I didn't want to lift it back up.

I collected the boys twenty minutes later though, made it back to the classroom and set them to work but it was a nightmare. The violent boy kept attacking others and some other boys had taken a cue from him and were beginning to niggle others as well. While I was giving them instructions, I just kept hearing the thought in my head, "Get me out of here. I don't want to do this any more. I don't know what to do to make them listen. Get me out of here."

Over and over. A new mantra.

The End

These were thoughts that were foreign to me and they scared me. I felt powerless.

Tired.

Numb.

Defeated.

The period lunch through to afternoon break was just as bad and I began to realise that I just couldn't do it any more. The boy who was causing heaps of trouble attacked a boy yet again and so I called to have him removed. One of the school counsellors came to collect him this time. When he came, I took a deep breath and took him aside to tell him how I was feeling. He kindly offered to cover me for the last lesson, so that I could see a deputy who was responsible for staff wellbeing.

I went to see the Deputy at the break and I told him how I was feeling. He said, "You need to put in a Workcover claim."

I was confused, fearful for the future and this sentence from out of the blue, hit me hard. I didn't know that as a relief teacher I could apply for Workcover. No-one had told me that I could. Looking back at it now, I find this incredible. If I had been a permanent staff member, my options most likely would have been made known to me. But because of the nature of my work, no one had given a thought about how I might be feeling and so I hadn't been told my options.

The deputy helped me to put a worker's compensation claim together, and, while we were completing it, the principal came in a few times. She showed some concern for me but encouragement like, "Sometimes we just have to put our head down and keep going," certainly didn't support me in the situation.

Whatever advice she offered, I felt it was too little, too late. I finished the claim and then drove to a psychologist's office near our house, where I had managed to schedule an emergency appointment.

I was finished.

First Appointment

"So you've now come to a very desperate place…."

The guy had summed it up in one sentence.

After I left school that day, I had headed straight to an emergency psychology appointment. The forty minute drive there had been a strange mixture of relief, apprehension, fear and excitement.

Relief, that I wouldn't have to go back to that school ever again.

Apprehension, about the approaching appointment. I had never ever been near a psychologist.

Fear for the financial future for me and my family.

But also, somewhat explicable, excitement because suddenly life had become an empty canvas. I dared to wonder what would be painted in the coming weeks because after all, it would only take a couple of weeks, right?

I arrived and was ushered in to Grant's office.

"So, what brings you here today, Andrew?"

I shared in a halting fashion about the events of the previous six weeks and Grant listened closely, occasionally jotting down notes but, in the main, sat in silence.

I stopped from time to time, gathering my thoughts and reigning in my emotions. The tissue box on the table was used well. In those times of silence between my sharing, as I blew my nose and wiped the tears from my eyes, I became acutely aware of the feelings that had been buried deeply inside and were pouring out of me freely, really for the first time. These emotions had been suppressed in the weeks after the incident, as I attempted to keep on working because I thought I had to. Now that I had found out that I didn't need to and that we would still be paid, suppression was no longer necessary.

In the six weeks leading up to this moment, all of these emotions had built and built and built, hundreds of kilometres out in the ocean: an event of seismic proportions had set a wave in motion which, unhindered, gathered strength and speed as it moved relentlessly towards the coast. Such was the force behind it that it could not be stopped. Once the event had occurred, this tsunami was destined to hit with full force. There was no other option.

I talked until I was spent. Until there were no more words, and we sat in silence, as Grant gathered his thoughts in an effort to summarise the tsunami in a succinct sentence.

"So you've now come to a very desperate place."

Someone understood. Even though I didn't at this stage, someone else did. There were no trite sayings, no advice about how to move on. Just nine words which summed up perfectly where I found myself.

A very desperate place…

A devastated shore line on a lonely beach. Wreckage and waste, what was left of a successful career, piled up on the sand, to be picked through by anyone who dared to wander along it.

Even now as I write, three years later, tears well up in my eyes as I think back on that moment. Grasping with all my might for an answer, for a way out of the darkness, for, ironically enough, a rope with which I could pull myself out of the pit I found myself in. But no matter how hard I pulled on that rope, my feet kept slipping on the muddy sides of the hole and I fell back down helplessly to rock bottom. I felt I was so far down, that as I leaned my head back and searched for the sky, for any hint of

First Appointment

moon or starlight (for surely it must be nighttime), all that I could discern was a mocking blackness, laughing openly at my plight.

Yes, it was a very desperate place and for now, even though Grant understood my plight, he was not the one who could pull me out yet. I was in too deep and there was work that I would have to do. But I sensed that he had been in a similar hole and that he had made it out, seemingly unscathed – though these sort of scars remain hidden. I had a feeling that he knew the way and could guide me safely out.

I cannot remember much else about that first appointment. I remember that sentence though. I remember that I recounted my experience. I remember having to fill out a questionnaire (more about that one later). But apart from that, I don't remember any details. I was in such a daze.

At the time, it felt like it had been the worst day of my life – the day that (I thought) I had reached the very lowest that I could possibly reach. Boy was I wrong about that, but at that point in time, as far as I was concerned, it was the bottom. The career that I had poured my life into passionately had come to a screaming halt. A temporary one, I thought, at that stage. I always thought I didn't define myself by what I did, and in the main I haven't. However that day, as the charred remains of my teaching career surrounded me, I certainly did.

It was indeed a very desperate place.

Interlude 1

"We live our lives oblivious to danger."
Someone said that to me recently.
Who knows how far from danger we are at any give time?
I had no idea at the beginning of THAT day
Or even halfway through the day
That I would enter into Azim's story
And play what would be a vital role
At a pivotal moment of his life

Would I have turned away from that moment
If I had known?
Would I had decided to let someone else follow him
And stayed in the classroom?
I don't know
On a superficial level
I would instantly say, "Of course not"
"Of course I would have acted in exactly the same way."

But here, almost six months later
In this dark, damp well
In which I find myself most days
With my teaching career seemingly over
With my passion to help people intact
But my desire to teach gone
With every area of my life it seems
affected in some way
With me having no idea of what the future now holds
In terms of career, vocation
I have to honestly answer right now,

Interlude 1

"I don't know."

Why?

I remember that question running through my mind the day that Azim attempted to kill himself.

Why?

"Why are you here? What has led you to this point in time, where you think that the only way to resolve the pain, the problems in your life, is to end it?"

A few weeks later I was asked to sit in a deputy's office, to be informed that Azim was not in fact attempting to end his life but merely acting out a game he had seen his mother play back in Sudan. So, according to the mental health powers that be, my question was invalid. There was no question to ask because what I thought he was trying to accomplish was not in fact occurring during those moments.

He was only playing. He had scaled up the 3 metre high side of some cricket nets because he had seen his mother do it. He had placed a noose around his neck because he had seen his mother do that. He had lowered himself over the side of the 3 metre high cricket nets because he had seen his still-living mother do this, or something similar, when he was growing up. He didn't have any deep questions, didn't have any problems that led him to this moment. It hadn't been necessary for me to act in the way that I did. He didn't need saving. Lowering himself over the edge of some cricket nets with a noose around his neck was a delightful game, with little chance that it would end in tragedy.

Of course....

Back to reality....

It was not the first time this "Why?" question had entered my head in such circumstances. You see, it was not my first encounter with attempted suicide. I will never forget a Friday night way back in 1993 – our first year of marriage. Sally had gone away with some female friends for the weekend and I found myself alone without her for the first time in our infant marriage. I twiddled my thumbs for a while that Friday night, not really knowing what to do. Being the first year of marriage, I had focused on building that relationship, to the exclusion of lots of other things during those first few months. Nothing unusual about that.

On that Friday night though, events happened which seemed beyond my control. It was one of those weird out of body experiences, where it feels as if you are watching someone else's life. I remember clearly the events, as I viewed them from above.

A young newly married man sits alone on a Friday, without his bride for the first time. He sits there in the half-darkened house, wondering what to do, when, before he can really sit and consider what to do, he picks up the White Pages ("What are they?" some readers ask), flips through the pages to find the correct letter, then searches for a name and number. As if on automatic, he dials (yes, dials) the number corresponding to the name he has located and sits there waiting for an answer, unaware of who it is he is ringing.

This is exactly how it transpired. To that point of my life, it was my eeriest moment. As a voice answered on the other end, I remember re-entering the world and clearly thinking, "Who am I ringing?" as the voice spoke.

"Hello?"

It seemed that I had called my friend Robert – an old high school friend with whom I had fallen out of touch during the years after high school, as he went his way and I headed to teach in the Northern Territory. When I came back to Adelaide after my northern sojourn, we had reconnected and contacted each other from time to time, and I had been able to invite he and his wife to our wedding. All now seemed peaceful in his life, despite a turbulent and frequently violent childhood and adolescence at the hands of a violent, abusive, alcoholic father. It seemed to me, albeit from a distance, that he had exorcised those demons.

That night on the phone however, when I asked him how he was, he uttered some words that I will never forget.

"How are you Robert?"

He replied. "Well, as a matter of fact, I have a shotgun in my hands and I am about to kill myself."

Whoa.

Twenty-one words that I will never forget. Funny: fast forward twenty-one years, to a day in 2014, and twenty-one life changing words were uttered by someone else I had only just met. The twenty-one words he uttered though were the precursor to an extraordinary event that pulled me out of a deep, dark hole that I realised later I had been in for decades. I digress.

I can't remember what happened in the moments after that really. I remember doing some quick talking and getting Robert to the point where he assured me that he would not in fact kill himself but would instead come over to our house for the weekend, since Sally was away.

As I drove over to his house though, admittedly extremely nervous, that question, "Why?" came to my mind.

How did your life lose its sanctity? How is that possible?

Life is either sacred… or it's not. Everyone's life is sacred… Or no one's is. There is no in between.

"What bought you to this place then, where your life was no longer seen by you as sacred?"

I drove over there with great trepidation coursing through my veins. Was it safe? Was I too late? Was this a wise move to be making?

I arrived, knocked nervously on the door and waited. It seemed to take an inordinate amount of time but eventually Robert opened the door and ushered me in. He looked gaunt; dull, lifeless eyes, face slack, and, not

Why?

just unsmiling, but showing little feeling at all. He was zombie-like, a walking dead, shrinking back from the fading sunlight for fear that he would truly be seen. Two decades later, I would understand perhaps a little of how he felt.

He invited me in. Nervously, I entered the house, glancing furtively left and right for any sign of the weapon of choice. There was nothing that I could see and I felt my jaw relaxing.

We sat down and chatted for a time about Robert's circumstances: a litany of seemingly logical reasons had led to the thankfully delayed decision that he had made. I will not go into them here, out of respect for all parties involved. Suffice to say though, that Robert came home with me that night and we spent the weekend working through his anguish. Thankfully his decision to end his life was put on hold for a time and Robert came and lived two doors down from us a short while later. He and I spent many late nights, talking about the sanctity of life, and jamming on our guitars. A healthy combination.

Sadly, despite my intervention on a number of other occasions – when Robert came close to going through with his decision – about a decade later he was eventually successful. The abuse of his childhood left visible scars on his back certainly but more so in his mind. The ones on his back seemed to be the easier ones to deal with. The scars in his mind – well, actually the gaping, putrid wounds in his mind, which would not heal, no matter how many self-help workshops he attended or books he read, could not be ignored. I believe it was these childhood unhealed wounds which led to the development of schizophrenia in his twenties and this was one enemy he could not fight on his own.

I am a lover of the *Lord of the Rings* movies. Yes, I know they're a world away from the novels, both in richness of language and the actual story but still. One of my favourite scenes, is when Frodo, who is beginning to have his eyes opened to the way the world really is, far away from the safety, comfort and peace of Hobbiton, seeks out the counsel of

Gandalf. He is beginning to ask, "Why?" He wonders aloud why the ring had to come to him. He questions why the responsibility falls to him – a seemingly insignificant cast member. He blurts out that he wishes the Ring had never come to him – that none of the events he finds himself a key player in had ever happened.

Gandalf listens carefully and then replies with an answer, which though wise, doesn't at the time satisfy all of the "why" thoughts Frodo was having. Gandalf gently counsels Frodo that he is not the only one to have these thoughts. They all have these questions with which they must wrestle and resolve. In the end however, all players have to decide, is what they do with the time that is given to them.

The "why me" question certainly came up when I was confronted with Robert's situation and again with Azim. But it's a redundant question. There is no answer to it that will ever satisfy. All I could do was decide what it was that I would do, both with my moments with Robert, years later with my few moments with Azim, and the incessant "Why?" that screamed silently to me in the years after the Azim incident.

Over the years Robert and I had many long conversations into the night about his battles with schizophrenia and the voices claiming to be from ten thousand years ago that tormented him. A comment he made which gave me comfort came one night, when he told me that when he was in our home, the voices that haunted and accused him vanished. Our decision to allow him into our home, despite the fears of the effect on, and safety of, our young family seemed to be vindicated because we were providing him sanctuary from accusatory voices.

I will never forget the last time he came to see me. That day he sat me down in our backyard and told me he had come to say goodbye and that if I heard down the track that "something had happened to him" to not worry. He thanked me for being his only friend and for standing with him, even after many in his family has disowned him. I had no words. Of course, once he left I called his mother to tell her that I feared for his safety and she called the appropriate authorities. A couple of months later, I learnt of his death.

I went to Robert's funeral. I felt I had to. I was the only friend who turned up. Close to my heart at his funeral, was the realisation that I had given him ten more years, during which time he was able to work through issues of faith and spirituality.

So, as I stared up at Azim, these thoughts came flooding back, albeit briefly. I thought of things that I may have said to Robert and wondered if anything that worked then, would work now. What would I decide to do with the time that I had? This was a totally different situation though. Azim was 11; Robert was a grown adult. Robert had laid down his method of choice by the time I arrived; Azim had his around his neck.

But again, "Why?" entered my head over and over again. I had no answers at the time.

And later, during my PTSD journey, as I ran the beach most mornings, that very same question ran through my head over and over, incessant, unceasing, relentless. It hunted me down, no matter how fast I ran. There was no way to outrun it. It was a cheetah, hungry for prey. It had marked me and it brought me down to the ground time and again, only to show seeming mercy at the last moment and set me free again. Or, perhaps I was its plaything.

My "Why?" was a different one to Azim's or Robert's. The "Why?" I asked on my beach wasn't to do with how they could possibly get to the point where taking their life was the only option. The "Why?" that pursued me down along the shore, day after day, kilometre after kilometre was more about why the Azim incident was haunting me; why couldn't I be free of it? Why did this incident have such a profound debilitating effect on me and why couldn't I shake it? I'm sure it was a question that others were asking also, from my dear wife to my psychiatrist.

You see I have always been a very deeply spiritual person. From a young age, I always felt that there was "more" out there than what we can see: that, in fact, what we see points to Something Else. I always believed that what we see around us points to something greater, something higher, something deeper. I always felt that I was playing a part in a Greater Story; and that the part that I was playing was an important part of that story, much the same as when Frodo and Sam discussed their parts in the story as they journeyed towards Mordor. I too was a hobbit: small but not so insignificant. Weak but having strength.

So as I ran my beach I wondered why it felt so empty now. There seemed to be no answers there, when before I could run the beach for hours and answer all of the world's problems it seemed. Now, there was nothing but "the question." It echoed back to me, as it bounced off the sandhills that stand as a Great Wall along so much of the South Coast. It bounced back, unanswered, almost mocking me and causing me to fall deeper and deeper into the depression that was dragging me into its dark, dank hole.

Looking back now, I can see that maybe sometimes there are no answers to this question. It's the one great burning question of humanity really. "Why do horrible things happen to good people?" We like to think that there is some cosmic logic to it all: that somewhere "up there" there is a gigantic, universal, eternal ledger book, in which we can look and see that, eventually, things do in fact tally up and so then, for some weird reason it makes what happened to us okay. As long as there is some sort of justice somewhere along the line to pay for what happened then we are willing to go through the pain of whatever situation we found ourselves in. Deep down, we feel that it has to make sense, otherwise it's just not fair and that doesn't make sense in this life. Deep down we know that it has to make sense; that truth and good and all that is decent must prevail. Otherwise, what's the point?

I suppose in the end, that's what kept me going: that, as Samwise Gamgee believed in LOTR, there is some good in this world, and it's worth fighting for. Thankfully for me, I could still stand in the hope that

Why?

Someone Else had done the fighting for me and that in One Great Act had balanced the ledger in my favour. That's what kept me going, despite the silence that I heard as the only reply to my question. If I hadn't found my answers in the silence, perhaps it was because I hadn't searched in the right places.

Perhaps that was what brought Azim and Robert to the place where the only answer was eternal silence: so that the questions would stop screaming at them. I don't know.

It was another question for which I had no answer.

Lessons from the Road #1

Sometimes when you're running
It seems as if
It's all you can do
To get to the next light pole
Or tree
Or house
Every step you take
Feels as if it's going to be the last one
For that day at least.

And so you focus
Just on that next light pole
Or tree
Or house
And sometimes
You even focus
On just the next step
Because that's all you can do
And then you focus
On the next step
And the next
And then another

And before long
You find that
By focusing just on that next step
Or the next light pole
Or tree
Or house

Lessons from the Road #1

You have taken more steps
And passed more light poles
And trees
And houses
Than you expected or realised
And that you've run further
Than you thought possible
On that run

And sometimes
This doesn't just apply to running ...

Learning to Fall

Our eldest son Josh is a brilliant artist. Self taught, he has never had extended tutoring. At the age of six or so, he just suddenly started drawing. His early efforts were not that great. Just scribbles really. You see, Josh had some really challenging developmental issues in a lot of areas, and still does. But despite his very real struggles, he kept at it and at it, for years and years.

It wasn't just with drawing either. One day, I remember it very clearly, I went into the lounge room to find Josh working intently on a construction with some Magnetix. Magnetix were quite popular for a time when he was young. Different polygon shapes, magnetic, which could be joined together to create all sorts of designs. The day I walked in, Josh had decided to build the Taj Mahal – from memory. Stunning.

Josh's gross motor skills were very slow to develop though. When he was finally up on his feet, it wasn't long before he was flat on his face. He had no reflexes, and as is the case with most toddlers in his exploration of the world, would develop lots of bruises because of his constant falling over. On our weekly hospital trips for all his other issues, we constantly received suspicious looks because of these bruises.

Because of his frequent face planting, the bruises as a consequence, and the subsequent suspicious looks during our hospital visits, my wife Sally had to teach Josh how to fall: to put his hands out in front of him, in order to protect himself from the fall. He had to be shown what to do so that he would no longer fall flat on his face as he tended to. Many demonstrations of falling over happened in our house. Sally would also have to move Josh's hands into the correct position. She had to be that explicit because on his own he just didn't know how to do it. He had to be taught how to fall down properly.

Falling over was a necessary part of his life you see, as it is with everyone. But he needed to learn how to do it properly. If he didn't learn to fall properly, then who knows, maybe one day he might not have wanted to rise again. As it was, he suffered from juvenile arthritis along with a myriad of other issues. Maybe the constant falling down incorrectly might have eventually taken its toll, and, even at his tender age, he might have decided to just stay down there.

In my dark hole, I knew exactly how he might have felt.

As I thought back on those days, I began to see something similar in my situation. I had fallen. Hard. Face planted. I had made it back to my feet fairly easily the first time. But what I found was that with every trigger; every school that I passed, or cricket net that I saw, or small child who crossed my path unexpectedly, I would face plant hard again. And again. And again. And again. Each time I made it back to my feet, I wondered what the point of it all was. "Why bother? I'm just going to be back down here again some time. Why not just stay down here? At least I'll be saving myself from another face plant."

And for a good deal of time, that's what I did. I didn't get back up again. Sick of the bruises, I stayed in bed. I didn't go outside. I withdrew from others. I didn't drive past schools. I avoided small children. I averted my eyes whenever I passed the cricket oval in town. I didn't drive anywhere near the school where the incident had occurred. It was just all too hard. I was always on edge. Always waiting for the trigger that would send me face first to the ground again.

I didn't know how to fall properly. I didn't have any reflexes. I had never been through anything like this before and I didn't have the skills I needed to save myself from the face plant. I couldn't walk through life with my hands constantly before me; that would just be silly but at the same time, the fight reflex dissipated a little more with each fall to the ground.

Another problem too was that I saw my falling down as failing. And both of these – falling and failing, are regarded as bad. Looking back now I see that failing and falling are a necessary part of growing. From my perspective now several years later, I have no regrets, no complaints about all that I went through. Without the falling, I wouldn't have died and risen again. The new life that sprouted from the death of so much of my old life has been stunning. My story, my perspective, sharing my wounds has helped so many other people with their seeming falling and failing.

I remember the night, though, when I sank to my lowest. I'm not going to go into details. Even now, thinking back three years later, I remember vividly the utter desolation of my heart and soul as I sat alone in the dead of night, among the ashes of a burnt out life. I couldn't go any further down. I knew it. I was at the end. I had no skills to get up again… I didn't want to… I was done. I felt I had face planted for the last time.

I sat alone there in the dark, at 3am, Elijah in a cave, wondering how on earth I would get up again, or if I even wanted to. I wasn't suicidal. Ending my life never crossed my mind. I had certainly reached a point where I could understand why other people would reach that decision. For me though, the sacredness of life held me secure. I didn't feel as if my life was mine to end. There were too many others invested in it, and denying them my life would cause them utter devastation and I could never do that to anyone.

But I was still lost. Utterly, completely lost. Helpless. Sick of face planting. I had no warning when the falls were about to happen. They came unexpectedly and I had no time to put my hands out and break my fall. Even if I did have a warning, I wasn't sure that I had the strength of will to put my hands out one more time to avoid the face plant. The reflex motion was gone. Muscle memory forgotten. Motor planning non existent. I was a blob, alone in the dark, with no inkling of how I could move from that spot, or even if I wanted to. It was utter darkness.

Somewhere else, I'm sure someone has called this "The dark night of the soul." I've been there. It's aptly named. It's dark.

And, that night, alone in the dark at 3am, it was utterly silent. Not a bird. Not a dog. The streets were silent. The roar of the Southern Ocean, always incessant where we live, could not be heard. And in that silence, even the questions that would scream at me as I daily ran my beach, were silent. My questioning of the events which led up to this time, the puzzle of why I could not shake the flashbacks or the trigger reactions all fell silent. I was done. This was the bottom.

And so, I sat there. Alone. In the dark.

But even then, that night, a tiny flicker of hope was rekindled.

There is a scene in the 80s movie *The Neverending Story* where Bastian, the main protagonist of the story has witnessed the destruction of Fantasia by "The Nothing." After the fury of the maelstrom, he and the Childlike Empress sit there, alone together, in the dark void. It seems to Bastian that she is all that remains of Fantasia. But she holds between her fingers a tiny glimmer. She says to Bastian that this tiny glimmer in her fingers in fact, is all that remains of Fantasia, and it is only with his help – with the power of his imagination and creativity, that it will be re-created.

"What are you going to wish for?" She asks.

A tiny glimmer remained for me that night too.

As I sat there in the dark, in my despair I opened my faithful iPad – which had been doubling as my brain for quite a few months by that stage – and turned to social media. It was 3am for me but not so in the US. I sent out a message to a friend whom I had never met in person but had spoken with regularly over the Internet. I regarded Judy as "my other mother"; a dear, dear friend with whom I felt that I could talk about anything and I knew that there would be complete, unconditional acceptance. We had lost touch a bit during the few years before this night. That's the way life is sometimes. But, just at the right moment, when I needed it desperately, Judy was there.

I shared my heart completely with Judy that night. Though the hour was late, I let it all spill out. I had nowhere else to go. No reflexes to prevent the face plant. No skills to lift me to my feet again. But thankfully at that moment, when I needed it the most, I found someone who was able to show me what to do.

You see Judy had been through pain too, albeit a different kind. We had shared that pain with each other over many conversations through the years. I had shown her my bruises from previous times when I had fallen down and wonder of wonders to me, she didn't look at me any differently because of them. She didn't think any less of me. In return, Judy had shared her pain and her bruises with me also and I tried, in my limited way, to accept her unconditionally as well. It was a unique relationship, a relationship of grace – unexpected – and one which I will always marvel at and treasure. I mourned for months when Judy died of cancer a few years ago.

With Judy's pain, instead of pushing it down and ignoring it; instead of staying down on the ground after she had fallen, she had pulled herself to her feet, time and again, and, as a result, she somehow knew what needed to be done to avoid the face plant. She was one who could teach me how to fall. In many ways, over the years, she had prepared me for this night. We had shared so much about deep things: our fears, our failures. So, I guess looking back, the skills were there for me. They had developed and were just waiting for the time when I needed to use them. Judy was the one, though, who needed to show me where to put my hands, and when to put them out so that I didn't face plant again.

Learning to Fall

I can't remember exactly what was said that night. I do remember hearing her reassurance that things wouldn't be as bad as they seemed in the cold dark of night. Honestly, I could not see any sort of future – in any area of my life. This was the bottom. But Judy could. She had not just fallen over and risen to her feet again. She had walked on from her falling down. She had continued on her journey and she could see a future for me, when all I could see was darkness. Most of all, she told me that I needed to sleep. I tried.

I woke in the morning still despairing, wondering if I could ever reclaim my life but with a Fantasia-like glimmer entrenched in my heart. That day, I spent a good deal of time facing a few hard truths.

What I saw most of all was that I needed further help. I had been seeing my psychologist weekly but it was not helping. I had also been keeping regular appointments with my GP. He had been suggesting medication but this was something I was emphatically refusing. I was an Aussie bloke. I was tough. I could beat this thing on my own. I didn't need any help.

I was wrong.

Medication

I stared down at the tiny light pink item in the palm of my perpetually sweaty hand. This is what it had come to. This was my salvation: the way that I would find my way back. Without it, my spiral downward would continue unhindered until I reached the very bottom of whatever hole I was in.

Medication.

The very word made me gag.

As a typical Aussie bloke, going to the doctor was hard enough. Let alone a psychiatrist. Let alone having a psychiatrist put me on medication. It went against everything I believed in as an Aussie bloke. I felt like I was letting the side down.

I stared at the tiny pill for the first time and I remember tears forming in my eyes. I thought mainly of the pain that I was causing my family, as they witnessed me literally and metaphorically staggering uncertainly from one day to the next, not knowing how they could help. I thought of the days and weeks and months that had passed with me not functioning much at all. I stared down at the pill. Was this really the answer to the questions screaming at me from my silent abyss?

It was one of those dramatic tension moments, where emotion is intensified by extended focus between actor and prop. Me and the pill. The pill and me. Front and centre with a full spotlight. Decision time. The audience hold their collective breath.

I took hold of my water bottle, placed the pill on my tongue, took a mouthful of water and swallowed. There. Simple. Problems over. Let's get on with life.

Medication

My GP warned me that in the days and weeks to follow, I "might" experience any number of symptoms. As it turned out, this was a huge underestimation.

Basically, if the symptom was mentioned on the label, I had it.

Nausea. Two weeks in, I remember waking up one morning and wishing I hadn't woken up. I had a psychology appointment that morning and I staggered into the room and collapsed into the plush seat, clutching my ever present thermo mug of tea. I didn't say anything. Grant took one look at me and commented, "You're green."

For some reason, I apologised for feeling sick. For two years following, waves of nausea washed not so gently over me. It was only ever the feeling of being sick, rather than the action, for which I, and I am guessing the rest of the family could still at least be thankful for.

Dizziness. This was the one which annoyed me most of all. It happened on and off during the day, every day for almost two years, and which resurfaces every so often even ten years later. It happened whenever I stood up, whenever I moved my head too suddenly, or whenever I changed direction. Running became agony. I would run but dizziness would engulf me and I found it difficult to run in a straight line. That year I attempted to run the 12km City-Bay. I ran the first half in one of my best times ever but, sure enough at the 7 kilometre mark, dizziness kicked in and to my dismay, I found it hard to run in a straight line. I'm sure I must have run twice the distance of everyone else. I resented that one of my very favourite things in the world had become such a chore.

Sweating. This occurred particularly at night. I seriously felt like I was incubating something: that some weird form of life requiring intense heat to grow and develop was growing inside of me. When sleep finally did find me, I would wake up in the middle of the night and find my pillow and sheets drenched in sweat, even in the middle of winter.

Trouble concentrating, memory problems. I felt like I was in a permanent stupor. I found it hard to string a coherent sentence together or remember even the most basic instructions from someone. For many years, I prided myself in knowing that I was the go to person when friends needed to fill a table for a quiz night. We had a pretty impressive record. But medication had the effect of not just dulling the senses of hopelessness and anxiety about the future, but every thought that I had. It didn't just dull the sadness, it dulled my ability to remember or feel anything. I felt like the walking dead.

Loss of appetite: this was a strange one. Because of the nausea I was experiencing, I rarely felt hungry. Despite this, I ate everything and anything, all the time. I lost my enjoyment for eating. I felt like my sense of taste was dulled. I started eating massive amounts of sugar.

Sleep problems. Nighttime was my nemesis. No matter what I tried in order to get to sleep each night, 2am would arrive and it had eluded me yet again. DVD sets became my greatest companion during those dark hours. I would watch hour after hour of some drama, wishing that sleep would find me.

I had been told that medication wasn't a cure for PTSD or depression but that being on it would simply give me a "break" from the dark hole I was experiencing. I was told that my mood would moderate while I was on it and that during this time, I would be able to pick up the skills I needed to properly manage PTSD and depression without the drugs.

In the end though I found that medication didn't do much for me at all really. I certainly didn't notice any moderation in my mood. Every time I went to the psychiatrist, he asked me how I was doing, I told him and his solution was simply to bump up the meds. Eventually, I was on the maximum dose of Pristiq (200 mg) and when on a subsequent visit to the psychiatrist, I reported no moderation, he added another drug in addition to what I was already on. My weight ballooned out by over 20kg and my blood pressure started doing weird things. It was such a concerning time for me and ironically, only added stress to what I was already experiencing.

Medication

So in order to self-medicate, I made sure I continued to run my beach. Despite the dizziness and nausea, despite the weight gain which was making everything harder. Despite the lack of sleep and the resultant weariness in the mornings, I committed myself to running the beach at 7:30 in the morning after I had dropped Sarah off at the school bus.

It was hard. Running was no longer the joy that it had always been but a chore. But as with the persistent southerly gale that winter of 2012, I pressed into the chore, determined to medicate myself in a way that the drugs weren't.

I was convinced that endorphins were the answer.

The Beach

Winter 2012 set in and I set my face, my will, all I had, to run the beach.

It makes perfect sense of course. The beach is always associated with the dead of winter. Especially our south coast with its bitingly cold southerly gales straight off the Antarctic.

Not.

But I have always loved running the beach. Whether it was back when were in Adelaide but even more so where we now lived. When we first arrived I was awestruck by the sight every time I visited the beach, whether that was the simple method of access by parking at the car park at the end of the aptly but sadly uncreatively named Beach Rd, or my preferred method in the early days, by driving along Barrage Rd to several non-designated parking spots, and then traversing half a kilometre or so of sandhills, usually with Maggie eagerly in tow. The vista that awaited after the sandhill trek never ceased to still me. Kilometre and kilometre of fresh white sand, and often during the week, not a soul to be seen in the direction that I took.

As I think back, running the beach in the dead of winter was an apt metaphor acknowledging my state of mind at the time. Bitterly cold. Windswept. Isolated. Pressing in to the incessant gale. That mirrored how I was feeling inside. Bitterly cold. Windswept. Isolated. Pressing in to the incessant gale of PTSD.

So I ran and as I did, more often than not, I listened to my music. On shuffle, as I shuffled, as I like to say.

But other times, particularly at the end of the run, I didn't listen to my music but the music that was already there around me. The music of the beach. At first, I didn't hear it. There was nothing but a full silence. But as the months passed, I began to listen to that full silence. And in the silence, the music of creation could be heard.

The Beach

I heard the wind in the silence. And in the wind, I could hear a symphony of sound that the wind made. Yes, actual wind instruments. The sound as it whipped off the ocean. The whistling as it blew through the soft sand. The howl as it came up against the sandhills of the south. The wrestle as the wind off the ocean met the whistling of the sand.

And above the sound of the wind, I could hear the ocean. And in the ocean, I could hear the original Water Music of the Creator. The incessant crashing waves. Waves crashing into the puddles pooling at the edge of water. The fizzing rush of waves turning to foam as they approached the shore and then the sound of foam dissipating as it reached puddles at the edge of water. The water returning to its source. Rivulets falling behind and scrambling to catch up.

As I leant into the silence of the beach during those winters especially, when most others were wrapped in quilts, or sipping their morning coffee by fires, I began to understand a bit more about the silence of the beach. And as I understood the silence of the beach, I began to press into and understand the silence in my soul, the silence of God. A silence so deep, that it seemed impossible for any sound to well up out of it. A silence from beyond deep time. Ancient, archaic, wise, pure, a silence from before the void and the chaos were even there.

This silence was there on the beach. This silence was there in my heart. This silence was there in my soul. Everything had been taken from my heart it seemed. Taken till it seemed there was nothing. Nothing to turn to, save to turn and face the silence.

The silence filled my ears until I couldn't hear anything.

However as the months went by on my beach of faith, I slowly began to understand that, just like the silence of the beach, the silence of God is anything but silent.

The Darkness

Darkness. It is morning. The sun has risen and is spreading its arms extravagantly across the day. Sally is up at first light and showering, ready for her teaching day. But in my PTSD world, there is darkness.

It is there from the moment that I wake. I say, wake, but really sleep has eluded me once again. There have been fitful bursts of it but, during those times, vivid nightmares have invaded my mind and awakened me.

I am a passenger in a car driving at high speed. We career out of control across an icy stretch of road and plunge helplessly and violently over a steep cliff and into the river below. As our car begins sinking, we try in vain to wind down the windows or open the car doors to escape…

I am a passenger on a plane. I am seated near the wings. I see the two engines on my side burst into flames and spread uncontrollably. We begin a steep descent. The oxygen masks fall down. I grab for mine and assume the crash position but I know it is futile. I have no control…

I usually wake with a start. Fully awake, alert, ready to take flight from, or fight, whatever danger awaits me. It has been that way, and increasingly so, in the days and months since Azim's suicide attempt.

Darkness.

It is there. I can feel it creeping over me, enveloping every part and snuffing out the sunshine. It is a deep, deep darkness, so deep that I feel smothered, unable to breathe. It is a true black hole, sucking all life into it, obliterating it, so that it is never seen again. Nothing survives a black hole and I know it is just a matter of time until I too fall helpless victim to it.

The Darkness

And most days, I don't care. I surrender willingly to the blackness. Arms outstretched in welcome, pleading to be swallowed up, so that I don't have to **feel** anymore.

Because if I allow it, I **feel** everything. It is as if every nerve fibre in my body has been stripped raw and exposed to the world, and every feeling is amplified by the rawness.

I cry at the drop of a hat.

I explode with anger at the slightest thing that goes wrong.

I panic in the kitchenware aisle of the supermarket, when I can't remember what to do next. I want to flee the store but know that I have to keep going.

I break out in a cold sweat when I pass a school, a playground, cricket nets.

I find it hard to look at or interact with young children.

I start to eat whatever, whenever. I had spent the beginning months of 2012 deliberating trying to lose weight. I had been really successful. I had cut back on eating junk, which I am so prone to do. I cut out chips – the bane of my life, lollies and bakery food. Bakery food, my friend, my comfort. I had lost almost 10kg and was feeling awesome.

All of that fell to the wayside as I sought comfort. The action of eating produced dopamine. Dopamine is a chemical which helps us to feel good and so I ate as much as I could, knowing that it was doing me no good physically but accepting gratefully and with arms (and mouth) wide open, the sugar kick as it hit my system…

The shower stops. I force myself now to get out of bed. I have given myself a few early morning jobs to do. Refill the filter jugs. Fill the kettle with water and boil it for Sally's morning coffee. Make Sally's lunch – salad with tuna or some other type of meat. She has been so good lately. Help Sally to take her school gear out to the car. Make Sarah's lunch if she wants me to. Take Sarah to the bus in time for it to leave at 7:25. Go for a run along the beach.

I still forced myself to run. It had become agony, a chore but I did it. Every morning for at least half an hour. I didn't enjoy it any more but I disciplined myself to do it. I knew that it was important – that if I didn't, then I would just be sucked up by the black hole and never be seen again. I wasn't that far gone that I didn't value my life. That would never happen. Never.

So, I struggled along the sand. Avoiding the wreckage and waste that was still lying there from the tsunami which had struck all those months ago. Running used to be such a joy but now…

Whenever I ran, invariably I would begin to feel nauseous. My legs and arms would turn to jelly and waves of dizziness would hit. These were all symptoms of PTSD and depression but later on, as I was prescribed medication, these symptoms, rather than dissipate, were amplified. It was awful. Truly, truly awful. But I struggled along the beach, remembering the days when I used to fly along it, and hoped beyond hope that those days would return and return quickly.

Back home. Shower. Drive to get the morning paper. Breakfast – usually muesli with yoghurt and decaf coffee. Then…

That was it. It was usually ten o'clock by now. But that was it for the day. It was here that I would hit the wall. It was here where the darkness would return and I would crawl back to bed and just lie there, sometimes sleeping but most often just lying there, staring out the window or at the ceiling. Maggie, my then six year old West Highland/Shih Tzu second best friend and newly discovered therapy tool would join me, snuggling near, as if she knew what was going on, providing comfort in the best way she knew how.

The Darkness

Hours would go by. I knew that the boys needed me. I was supposedly homeschooling them that year but my supervision had quickly fallen by the wayside. I was still programming work for them but there was little assistance given and my checking of their work had dissipated.

I just couldn't think any more. My thoughts were jumbled at best. An amorphous blob at worst. When I tried speaking, I had trouble stringing two coherent sentences together. Reading, one of the joys of my life, slipped away, well out of grasp. I tried, but could barely manage a page. When I did manage a page, comprehension was non existent. Recall even more so.

Dizziness became a major concern for me. My doctor said that because of the medication I was on, my blood pressure was affected. It was normal when I was sitting down, but every time I stood up, it plummeted, which for me meant that waves of dizziness would hit me. I'm sure Tim thought I was going to pass out on many occasions, as he watched me coming out of the bedroom with an entirely vacant expression and wavering on the brink of collapse. It would hit me wherever, whenever and it scared me. I would be talking to a person, turn my head or my body a certain way and then be on the brink of fainting…

But there was a part of the darkness that I hated and feared the most.

It was the utter, complete feeling of helplessness and hopelessness that engulfed me.

I felt I had no defence to the waves of blackness which had enveloped me. I was powerless. Every time it hit, I fell to the canvas and each hit saw me stay down for longer and longer. The final 10 count never came though. I longed for it because then I could stay down. I didn't want to get up and face my adversary any more.

I could see no future. I was stuck in the past, replaying the incident over and over and over. The DVD player/recorder ("What is that?" I hear some readers ask) was stuck on rewind. I would play it, rewind it, and play it again, often in slow motion during the most horrific parts. And I couldn't help but watch. My mind still couldn't fathom how such an event was possible at such an innocent place as a school. As one teacher there that day had said to me, "That's the worst thing that I've ever seen at a school." That helped me to a degree to process it. It confirmed for me that it wasn't my imagination. It really did happen and it was bad. But the hopelessness remained. I could no longer see a future – certainly not in teaching, and my mind grappled with my ability to function in any job.

Three o'clock came and each day I struggled out of bed to try to do the basics: laundry, dishes, sweeping and preparing the evening meal. I needed some sort of structure to my day but this was all I could manage at this stage. These tasks took me a long time to complete and left me exhausted.

Five o'clock arrived and I knew each day that Sally would soon be home. This was the highlight of my day. I would listen for the chugging of our van and then go outside and help her with all of her gear. She was struggling at school with various issues and so I appreciated being able to listen to her and even, shock, horror, make some suggestions that might help.

The evening would be filled with helping her with anything that she needed to prepare for the next day, walking the dog and any taxi driving with the kids. Driving the kids places was good. My mind focused on the road and nothing else. I was able to do that and, even though it might only be for half an hour or so, switch off the DVD player in my head. Then, often because I had to wait for Sarah to finish with her rehearsal, I would lie there with my eyes closed, thankful for some dozing time. Not deep enough for REM sleep and dreaming. Just dozing. That was safe.

And then I would drive home and crawl wearily into bed. Sally was always exhausted, understandably so. We chatted for a while and then she would fall into a deep, welcome sleep whilst I watched on, envious. Through the dark watches of the night, I longed for such a sleep but at

The Darkness

the same time, was fearful of it. Deep sleep brought disturbing dreams and I didn't want anything to do with them. On the other hand, I was exhausted and longed for the sleep that I could see Sally was enjoying. And so, I found myself in the classic catch-22 situation: wanting sleep but fearing it. Eventually, as my eyes grew heavy, I half welcomed what was approaching. However, I knew that a greater darkness would be waiting for me again in the morning…

Interlude 2

(Because it's all been a bit heavy up to this point)

The Waiting Room Handbook: An etiquette guide for Psychologists' Waiting Rooms

Rule no. 1
You must not make eye contact

Rule no. 2
You must not sit too close to someone else

Rule no. 3
You must not engage in conversation with someone else (Are you sure they're actually there?)

Rule no. 4
You must not smile

Rule no. 5
You must not sit on someone else's chair

Rule no. 6
You must not bring small children

Rule no. 7
Do not touch the dial on the radio

Rule no. 8

Interlude 2

Do not tell any jokes

Rule no. 9
Do not wave goodbye to the previous patient.

Rule no. 10
Do not think about funny things

A Song not Scored for Breathing

"I will hold you."

"I will not let you fall."

"I will not let you go."

"If you let go, I will catch you."

Over and over. A mantra. Convincing myself that this would be the way of the world. Certain that if I repeated it enough, then it would be so.

Looking up at those desperate eyes, filled with visual memories of unimaginable horrors that I could not even begin to reproduce in my mind. Realising that I was blocking him from his solution and this was why those eyes were also filled with complete hatred seemingly towards me.

"I will not let you fall."

"I will not let you go."

As it turned out, the mantra was true. It was a self fulfilling prophecy. I said it, and it came to pass. You see, I did hold on to Azim. And I didn't let him go. In the end, I held on to him for two years.

"I will not let you fall."

"I will not let you go."

A Song not Scored for Breathing

Three months later, I wanted someone to utter the same words to me. Three months later, I was the one on top of the crickets nets looking down: with a noose knotted with memories that wrapped not only around my neck but also wound down around my body with the rest of the rope. It held tight and would not let me go: a python of depression wrapped around me whose constrictions were strengthening; a potential energy build-up which would eventually send me over the edge, and cause me to choke on the vividness of the pictures which flooded my mind, day after, hour after hour, minute after minute, second after second.

"I will not let you fall."

"I will not let you go."

Search as I might, aside from my family, there was no friend that I could find, willing to stand under me as I had done for Azim at the cricket nets to catch me whenever I fell. Of course, my wife was always there. Of course, my kids were there. But sometimes, family is too close and you need someone else removed from the situation to come in and be the support. The pressure on the immediate family is too great and it does the person struggling nor the surrounding family any good in the long term. Pain that is not transformed is transmitted and much damage can be done that also needs to be dealt with, probably not until the PTSD and depression have subsided.

But I had no one who was prepared to come alongside. The sad thing about this is I was an active member of my church, where I was involved in worship, either leading or playing every week. I continued this all through my struggle for a year or so. I believed that worship was not just about being happy-clappy but also about worshipping God when things were not going so well. I was Joseph, the boy with a coat of many colours, sitting forgotten in the dungeon, wondering if I would be remembered. I was Job, who had seemingly lost everything, sitting in ashes, worshipping his Creator, acknowledging that all belonged to Him. I was very open with my struggle in worship. I believed that being real was important.

"I will not let you fall."

"I will not let you go."

That's what I longed for each time I shared. But no one came underneath to be there to catch me. Every now and then, someone at church would say "hi" during the frantic coffee time afterwards and ask me how I was. I would tell them …

Not pouring out my heart but just an honest reply in a sentence or two. There would be an awkward silence, a shuffling of feet, a sip or two of coffee and then perhaps some attempt at a reply. An explanation about why I was feeling this way or had I tried something else. But this is not what I needed. I needed someone to breathe for me for a while.

I've heard that way back in the history of music, before the Renaissance perhaps, there was a certain type of song which had the instructions, "A song not scored for breathing." I've hunted in vain for more information about this but it seems that most Choral works often had breath marks (') indicating who should breathe (sopranos, altos etc) and when. However, this "song not scored for breathing" was different. It didn't have any indication of who should take a breath and when. Members of the choir breathed when they needed to.

The effect of this was that, unlike other songs that were scored for breathing where audiences could hear the pauses for breath, in this unique type of scoring, the audience were not able to detect those pauses. It was just one continuous sound. Overall, it seemed that there was no time to stop to breathe. Underneath, however, each chorister breathed when they needed and the other members of the choir carried the song forward until they too needed to breathe. Each choir member breathed when they needed, and the rest carried the burden.

And that's what I needed. I was exhausted. Breathless. Cyanotic. Turning blue for lack of oxygen. Not brain-dead but getting there. The load I was carrying; the constant replays in my head, the fatigue, the nausea, the worry that financially we might go under, even though I was "compensated" through Workcover, was sending me down time and time again. I needed someone to breathe for me for a while, to take the strain, to carry my cross. I couldn't do it any more.

But try as I might, I couldn't find anyone in my immediate geographical area who would be that person for me. I had friends overseas that I spoke with regularly online but I needed people who were physically present. I needed people apart from my family who would be there with me, without judgement or expectation, in the deep, dark hole. This part of my story was vital and I needed people, or at least one person, willing to take their place beside me, and help me fight. I needed a fellowship.

One of the things that impacted me when I watched *The Lord of the Rings* movies was the fellowship the friends developed. It's a strange word – one that is used often in church circles regularly but I'm not sure if it's well understood. The word "fellowship" is defined in various places in a number of ways including, "a community of interest, activity, feeling or experience," "a company of equals," "the quality or state of being comradely" and "meaningful communication for building trust." I wanted all of these things. I wanted someone who would do community with me through the experience of my darkness; someone who would walk beside me as a comrade with a shared goal and not look down on me because of what I was going through but hold me in equal regard as themselves. I wanted people who would go with me through the darkness on a quest to Mt Doom.

The diverse group in the LOTR movies were thrown together, but thrown together for a common cause. The one ring. Its destruction. The future of Middle Earth depended upon this group of creatures working together, despite their differences. At the beginning, their differences created raw wounds, as they rubbed against each other. But as time passed, as some of them died or were separated, those who remained learnt that their survival and that of a larger story, depended upon them giving their all for each other.

"I will not let you fall."

"I will not let you go."

That's what the LOTR fellowship said to each other with their lives. It was gutsy, true fellowship. That's what I wanted to hear. I needed someone to breathe for me for a while.

Interlude 2

Friends

Where are you?
Now is the time
When I need you the most
Not to talk to
Not to hear what you think I need to hear
Not even to listen to me
I just need you to be here
To be a companion
To be by my side
In silence even
Someone there by my side
To hold me up
When the waves of dizziness and nausea and depression hit
Someone to pick me up again
When they become too much for me to bear
And I collapse in a heap where a few moments earlier
I seemed to be functioning normally

And I need your time
I need to know that when you ask me, "How are you?"
And I tell you exactly how I am
You'll come back
And ask me again the next time we meet

Because believe me
I've seen so many pairs of eyes glaze over
I've seen the disinterest

The eyes wandering, looking for another place to be
When I let them know
How I really am
Rather than the standard, trite reply

I'm looking for something deeper
Than just the surface
I guess because if I had just done the surface stuff
With Azim
Someone else would have found him swinging
If I hadn't gone to the lengths I did
To find out how he was
No one would have had the opportunity
Instead they would have been mourning the loss
Of a lovely yet troubled boy
"We had no idea he was going through any of that"
That's what they would have said about him

It's not something that I want said of me…

Life on a Scale

"I found myself getting upset by trivial things."
"Three."

"I was aware of dryness of my mouth."
"Oh, three."

"I experienced breathing difficulty (for example, excessively rapid breathing, breathlessness in the absence of physical exertion)"
"Zero."

"I just couldn't seem to get going."
"Three."

"I had a feeling of shakiness (eg, legs going to give way)"
"Three."

"I couldn't seem to get any enjoyment out of the things I did."
"Two."

And so it began again. Rating my mood, my life, on a sliding scale of 0 to 3. It was something that happened every time and this process itself was beginning to get me down. With every 'two' and 'three', I felt a wince inside. It was like a sharp dagger being twisted into my heart every time I called out a number. This was the roll call of my week; the litany of symptoms and moods that dominated my thoughts and kept me tied down, unable to move anywhere. I seriously wanted to be absent, to call in sick.

Of course, I could have been dishonest and called out a different number but what was the sense of that? I had the feeling though that Grant would know. He was no fool.

"I felt I was close to panic."
"Two."

"I found that I was very irritable."
"Three."

"I feared that I would be "thrown" by some trivial but unfamiliar task."
"Three."

I was not sure what to think of these sessions. I seemed to come away from them with an even darker cloud over me than when I went in. A few people had warned me of this: people who had been through a similar event to me and had to attend counselling. They had said that they tied themselves up in knots before the session, thinking about all they might bring up, and then during the session it would all spill out, or something new might come up which needed to be processed, and then they would come away totally spent.

"I tended to overreact to situations."
"Two."

"I experienced trembling (in the hands)."
"Two."

"I found it difficult to relax."
"You're kidding, right? Three."

Life on a Scale

Difficult to relax? These sessions didn't seem to be helping me at all. All they seemed to do was dredge it up over and over, with the effect of sending my mind into turmoil yet again. The problem was that I found it so hard to think, and thinking was demanded of me during the session. I didn't want to think. I just wanted to curl up into a tiny ball and be left alone. The demands placed on my brain were so severe that I would arrive home from a session, disoriented and so, so down. I would just grab Maggie, my dog, therapy tool and second best friend, go into my room, shut the door, climb up into our bed with Maggie and just hug her until I fell asleep. I would sleep for several hours and then wake suddenly, rudely, with the remains of the session still echoing in my head.

"I felt that I was using a lot of nervous energy."
"Energy? Zero."

"I felt down-hearted and blue."
"Three."

"I felt that I had nothing to look forward to."
"Three."

"I was intolerant of anything that kept me from getting on with what I was doing."
"Doing?... Zero."

By the time I staggered out of my bedroom, and reoriented myself after the waves of dizziness that would engulf me, it would be 3 in the afternoon. I would force myself out of that room and make myself put on a smile, do some dishes, clean the kitchen and hang out clothes. Then I would make some tea, and wait for Sally to come home, so that I could help her with whatever work she had to complete for the next day. It was a routine. Not a very positive or productive one but a routine nonetheless. Helping Sally helped me too. I felt that being able to do something for her, whether that be preparing or printing or listening or giving advice about a student, gave me some sense of normality.

"I was unable to become enthusiastic about anything."
"Two."

"I felt I was close to panic."
"The rice and pasta aisle in Woolies. Driving past an oval. Seeing a child. Cricket nets. Schools… 'Three' isn't high enough."

"I felt scared without any good reason."
"Three."

But the feeling of satisfaction from helping Sally out didn't last that long. Truth was, I did fear for the future. Even more, I was scared because I couldn't even see a productive future for me any more. Stepping out of the door, the bedroom door, let along the front door required so much effort. It was an achievement but when I stood it up against previous achievements in my life, well…

"I felt I wasn't worth much as a person."
"What? No, never. Zero."

"I felt that life was meaningless."
"Oh no, zero."

But those two were there at the end, every single time. These two stood out above all the others. For even in my darkness, in the silence of major depression and PTSD, these two descriptors of my self-rating always scored a zero. Always. Because, even in the depths, I saw that I was not a zero. I somehow still clung tenaciously to the ideal, planted deep within me that I was worth something; that my life though presently disintegrated, would some day in the future become reintegrated and I would see beauty and meaning rise from the ashes. It was a belief planted firmly in my soul and no matter how deep down I went into depression, it was these two which kept me from the abyss.

These two thoughts – that I was worthy as a person and that my life had meaning, were a throwback to that first silent night on the South Coast, as we lay there together on our backs.

I remembered that silence – lying there, in the dark, breathing in its deliciousness. I remembered how I thought, "This is what I need. This I where I'm meant to be. I belong here. This is what I've been searching for. I've come home." I remembered in my depths, that in the silence on the first night, I could sense peace and rest. In that silence, I had felt safe and secure. In that silence, I had found the answers to questions that I had been searching for, for a lifetime.

And so, as I rated my life on a scale, though it drove me down, when those two questions were asked, I took my mind back to the silence of that first night and tried to breathe it in again.

I listened to that silence. That silence was good. It was very good.

The Apple Tree: a Parable

When we made the decision to quit city life and move to the country, we hunted high and low for a great location. We eventually settled on a two and a half acre block, on an island, in the middle of a river. It was connected to the mainland by a bridge. The river mouth was not far from us, so we felt we had the best of all worlds: a country location, a river, an island, but connected to the mainland, close to the sea and the hills. And really not so far from civilisation.

So, we bit the bullet and bought the block. To celebrate the occasion, I bought some fruit trees – two apple trees, a lemon and a cherry, and with a great sense of ceremony and a good deal more naïveté, I took the boys along with a friend of ours down to the block to do a ceremonial planting. I had romantic notions of settlers taming the wilderness and staking out a claim for the land. We had even brought shovels and matches!

It was a cold, foggy day. The air was still though and we had planned to build a campfire and cook some sausages. It was a real boys' day out. We arrived midway through the morning and, after the most important task – a visit to the bakery – had been completed, we drove over the bridge to our soon-to-be island home. I took the chain off the gate with a flourish and drove onto the block. It was the middle of winter, so the grass was green and shin high.

We decided to plant first and eat later.

I took the shovel and walked over to the place where I had planned to plant these, soon-to-be orchard trees. I asked one of the boys to preserve this moment forever on camera. I dug into the soil – rich and brown.

"Hey, great top soil!" our friend commented. I felt immensely proud, as if it was due to my efforts in some way that the soil was so good. I kept digging, visions of a not-too-distant future lush, productive orchard filling my mind.

"Clunk!"

About fifty centimetres down, I hit rock. Limestone. "Never mind," I thought. "I'll just try somewhere else."

So I tried a spot a few metres from where I had first dug.

"Clunk!" same result.

Undeterred, I tried again and again in several different locations around our two and a half acre pride and joy. Each time, we started out with promise, believing that this time, we would have success. But to no avail.

Eventually, we found a spot where there seemed to be a little more topsoil and, with a heart throbbing a little less strongly and proudly, planted our two apple trees, lemon tree and cherry tree. We told them to live longer and prosper, did our guy stuff with fire and sausages and then left.

Of course, I hadn't thought of how I would care for this future flourishing orchard. The water connection for the block was a hundred and seventy metres down the other end of the block and there was no way that we could afford yet to pay for the blueline pipe that we needed to run from the mains to where we had planned to build our house at the other end. It was early June when we planted, so they would be fine through winter and spring…

But summer was coming.

We moved down to the island the week before Christmas 2008 and rented a house not far from our block. We visited the block quite regularly because we were discovering that some things were able to grow and indeed flourish in only half a metre of topsoil. They were called weeds. We had no lawnmower, so once the block had been slashed the only choice we had, was to pull out the hundreds of three corner jack weeds that sprang up by hand. The fruit trees that we had planted so proudly five months before were soon choked by hundreds of weeds of every description. We did our best though and the trees seemed to survive.

But there was more.

2008/2009 was a dry, dry period in Australia. Many described it as the worst drought ever. The Millennium Drought. The river that our island was nestled in, the Murray, was in dire trouble. A water source to much of the nation, it was under severe stress and as we were down the bottom of the river, we began to see and feel the effects first of all. A river always dies from the bottom up, and die it did. Bit by bit, the river receded for the first time in living memory to reveal the ancient, sandy riverbed. Eventually, it was possible to walk along it for kilometres. Dry, acidic sand, punctuated here and there with areas of thick, gooey, smelly mudholes, where you sank down to your knees. There were fears that when the hot northerly wind blew, it would blow acidic sand into the gutters of surrounding houses, which, when it did finally rain, would flow into the rainwater tanks of residents on the island and elsewhere.

Of course, the effect of this on our yet-to-be-established fruit trees was dire. Buffeted by hot northerlies, possibly the hottest ever experienced in that area, and deprived of life giving water, the cherry tree was the first to go. Never meant to be planted in such a hostile environment, the fragile sapling went quickly. One of the apple trees followed soon afterwards, followed a few weeks later by the lemon tree. It was a depressing sight. Dreams of living off the land, of visiting the orchard daily to pick of its bounties were soon swept away by the reality of the northerlies that whipped up the acidic sand of the river bed and sent it over our precious block.

One symbol of hope remained. A solitary apple tree. The blossoms and leaves also shrivelled and died, as did the young fruit which it had somehow managed to produce despite the extreme stress. Its branches

The Apple Tree: a Parable

were now bare but they still showed traces of green, rather than the dry cracked brown of its now dead companions.

But despite the traces of green and perhaps because of the shared dismay of our new town, as we together grieved the dying of the river, disillusioned, I gave up on that apple tree. I left it in the ground though: a symbol, perhaps, of something that I wasn't quite sure of.

The rains finally came the following winter and the drought of all droughts broke. Water returned to the river and, as spring approached, we decided to begin a planting programme. We found a group nearby who propagated plants native to the island, and, wanting to stay true to that, bought up big. During the last weeks of winter and the first few of spring, we planted almost 100 trees, mainly along our northern and western boundaries, in a bid to create a windbreak for coming summers.

One day, as I was busily planting, I happened to come across the apple tree that I had left in the ground. It was surrounded by weeds, and covered in hundreds and hundreds of tiny snails. The snails had been there so long, they had become encrusted on the thin trunk and branches of the tree, much as barnacles on the bottom of a boat.

Out of curiosity and perhaps sympathy, I began to peel off the snails. It was a thick, gooey mess. Quite disgusting really. But as the snails began to come away from the trunk, I saw that there were signs of life in that apple tree. Despite the remains of shell which could not and would never be removed, the young thin trunk was still a healthy browny-green colour, not shrivelled and lifeless at all. There was hope.

I managed to scrape away most of the snails and then proceeded to clear the weeds away from the surrounding soil. I fertilised and watered it, and continued to water it on a daily basis through spring.

Soon more signs of life appeared. Leaves budded on the previously bare branches. Then, wonder of wonders, blossom appeared. A few dozen soft pink flowers bloomed on the tree but of course died away as there wasn't another apple tree nearby to cross pollinate with.

Through that spring though, the apple tree continued to thrive. Summer arrived and the leaves fell off but the following winter and spring I looked again and was amazed to see further signs of life and growth. I continued to weed and water and fertilise and keep the snails at bay, and against all the odds, it continued to grow. A short, stumpy apple tree with branches starting barely a few centimetres from the ground but an apple tree nonetheless.

That apple tree has been planted there for thirteen years now and shows no sign of dying. It still bears the scars of its ordeal though. They will never fade I feel. It may never grow to its full height either. It hasn't borne any fruit yet but as of this spring it now has a partner. In time, when it is ready, when it has recovered from the trauma of drought and weeds and poor soil and hot winds, I have high hopes that it will cross pollinate and produce a sweet, sweet crop of its own and help the other tree to produce a crop also.

And I hope that, when the time is right, when drought and stifling northerlies subside, the same will be true of my life.

Dead Air

"Andrew, I want you to think about something."

"Ok."

"I want you to imagine that you are your best and wisest friend."

"Right…"

"If you were your best and wisest friend, what sort of advice would you be giving yourself?"

"Wow. Umm… I don't know. Stop talking to myself?"

"Ha… Now this is serious. Your mood has been down for a long time now – nine months. Is it fair to say that you expected that this would only last a few weeks, or maybe a month?"

"Oh yes… Absolutely. I feel just ridiculous…"

"If it was someone else. What would you say to them?"

Words came so slowly to me during this time of my life. I found it so hard to string two words together, let alone a sentence or two. The effects of huge amounts of drugs on my system had dulled my ability to think dramatically. But I gave it my best shot.

"Well… To be honest… I don't think I would say anything… I would just listen… and make sure that I heard properly… That's what I find… annoying. Whenever someone talks to me… I just wish that they wouldn't… give me their opinion… of what they think I need. Sometimes… they listen… but they don't really hear… They don't… put themselves in my shoes… You know that line from *To Kill a Mockingbird*? "Walk a mile in someone's shoes?"… Remember that?… Well, it's like that… but in reverse… It's almost like they put me… into THEIR shoes… and the advice that they give… is more about what THEY would do… if they were me… It's advice that is often thoughtless… and tactless… I just wish there was someone apart from my wife… who would commit to me… who would spend time by my side… as a friend… and not just act… as if they know what I need."

"Often that does happen with people. They feel like if there is empty air that it needs to be filled up with something. A bit like dead air on radio. Silence is uncomfortable to most people."

"Yes… But often it's that dead air… that silence… that I'm craving… There is so much noise… going on… All day… every day… I just want to hear… nothing… And to have someone… who will sit with me… without judgement… without expectation … in the silence… "

There was silence… I grabbed a tissue, wiped my eyes and sipped from my thermo mug. We just sat there, Grant and I for a good two minutes, not saying anything.

Silence. There it was, just for a moment. A silence that didn't scream at me. A silence that wasn't full of questions. A silence that wasn't a void, empty of all hope. It was silence that held promise, just for a moment. It was the silence of that first night down on the south coast, where my wife and I lay in the darkness just listening. Listening to the promise of what was to come.

For a moment, the voices, the feelings, the dark cloud dissipated and the sky was blue. For a moment, there was a hint of hope. The glimmer of Fantasia. I'm sure I caught a glimpse of it from the corner of my eye. It made a sudden movement to catch my attention. Yes, there it was… And then it was gone…

In my heart I knew it was only respite, rest for a moment but I so appreciated that moment because it gave a moment's rest but it also held promise – oh, God I hoped, of things to come.

Grant looked at me again. "So Andrew. Again, if you were you best and wisest friend, what advice would you be telling yourself?"

"… I would say… Andrew, give yourself time… and be gentle on yourself."

"Yes."

Interlude 4

Amidst all the noise
All I was searching for
Was silence

Silence from the chatter
Of psychiatrists and the doctors
And rehab people
Telling me what I should be doing
And how I shouldn't be feeling this way anymore

Silence from the scream in my head
That sounded out
All day every day

Silence from the ringing in my ears
One of the few constants in my life
Thanks to medication

Silence from the endless replay
Of the incident
Over and over
Every detail
In high definition

Silence from the questions
So many questions

Wounded Healer

We came across it as I was driving Sarah home from yet another rehearsal, for yet another production, late one night. We arrived at the turnoff for the winding road that leads home.

I love driving that road. The anticipation of knowing that the home stretch has been reached is always palpable with me. And as we get closer to home, and descend through the hills, there are several teasing views of that which awaits us. Our cosy town, our island home, the majestic view of the river as it embraces the island and then releases as it flows to the sea, the lake off in the distance, the thin line of sand dunes and beach which separate the river from the Southern Ocean, and the ocean itself, which stretches south for thousands of kilometres before it reaches the Antarctic. When the cold southerly blows in winter though, you would swear it was closer.

Anyway, we had almost reached this turnoff when we came upon a sad scene. There was a group of two or three cars, headlights still on, engines running on the other side of the road. The occupants of those cars had congregated in a semi circle on the median strip of the two lane road. As we slowed to turn off, I could make out the subject of their attention. It was a kangaroo.

The poor creature had been hit by one of the cars and was now lying on the road, one or both back legs obviously broken. I too stopped the car and went out to see if there was anything that could be done.

As the others present discussed what to do, I couldn't take my eyes off the kangaroo. It was trying desperately to escape, using its tiny, weak front paws, certainly not created for such a task, to drag itself away from the people trying to help it. I looked into its eyes and could somehow sense its feeling of pain. And, for some reason that I couldn't understand at the time, I could identify with it too. Weird, I know.

Wounded Healer

I thought about it over a period of weeks. I couldn't shake the image of the kangaroo's pain-filled eyes from my head. I wondered if the pain that was running rampant in my heart and head, found an outlet to the world through my eyes. Could others see the pain that I was feeling, just as I could see it in that poor creature?

Most of the time, though I felt in pain, I thought it was something that only I could sense. It couldn't be seen. It wasn't like a physical impairment, such as a broken leg. An injury such as that always evoked a response from people, either by spoken word, or the obligatory signing of the cast. But no one could sign my cast. No one could reach it, let alone write on it. If they could though, I wondered what they would write on it.

Get well soon

Chin up

Stay strong

Just forget about it and move on

All very nice but not very helpful. All they did was make the wound more noticeable and remind me of how far I had fallen.

The kangaroo had been wounded. It was no longer able to do what it had been designed to do, which was to hop freely on its strong back legs throughout the Aussie bush and occasionally create havoc with traffic. I wondered if it would ever be able to do that again: to be rehabilitated to such a point where it could be set loose to run, or rather hop, amok across the countryside, or whether it would be confined for the rest of its days in some sanctuary for rescued fauna. Sanctuary in terms of rest, certainly. However, in terms of being made whole again, so that it could take up its former life, then no.

Silence: A Spiritual Journey Through PTSD

Wounded. Not able to do what it was created to do.

During this time, I felt like that. Wounded. In desperate need of healing from someone, so that I too would not have to drag myself along at a pitiful and ultimately futile pace to seeming safety. At times, I felt that the blood, the life in me, had drained away and that I had reached a critically low level of loss, from which no amount of transfusions would restore vitality to my system.

Wounded. No longer able to do what I had been created to do.

Teaching seemed forever away. I could not see a way back to it. Even almost two years later, passing a school could sometimes trigger a flashback. There were times when panic attacks would still hit me in the frozen food section of the local supermarket. That sniper was still there, waiting for me and I still couldn't deal with the resulting chaos in my heart. As a result of this, I just could not see the point in pushing a return to teaching any more. It just would not be a healthy, wise choice to make.

But I knew deep down that helping people through stuff was my thing. I knew that I had helped countless children over the years, through both my teaching in schools and my after-hours theatre company. So many children. Some had deep hurts, be that due to abuse or a syndrome or condition that they were born with, or a stutter, or a learning difficulty or whatever.

I had helped them. I had seen them. I had accepted them and I had aided in the healing process. I had a part to play and at times it had been a leading role. But now, I was wounded. How could I ever hope to help heal others ever again? It seemed so, so far away.

The American playwright, Thornton Wilder wrote a one act play, entitled *The Angel that Troubled the Waters*. It was a play based on the

Wounded Healer

Biblical account of the Pool of Bethsaida in ancient Jerusalem. The pool was claimed to contain healing powers, brought about by an angel, who every so often would come and stir the water. The locals said that the first person into the pool after this occurrence was often healed, and so many people gathered in expectation, hoping to be the first.

The main character in the play is a doctor. This doctor, named "The Newcomer", suffers from depression (or melancholy). Though a healer in the eyes of many people, he comes to the pool, hoping, like the others, to be healed of his condition.

An angel does appear, but before he stirs the waters, he commands the doctor to stay back. The doctor pleads with him for mercy, for healing. But the angel says that the moment is not for him but for someone else. What follows is the dialogue between the doctor and the angel:

The Angel: "*Draw back, physician, this moment is not for you.*"

The Newcomer: "*Angelic visitor, I pray thee, listen to my prayer.*

The Angel: "*Healing is not for you.*"

The Newcomer: "*Surely, surely, the angels are wise. Surely, O Prince, you are not deceived by my apparent wholeness. Your eyes can see the nets in which my wings are caught; the sin into which all my endeavors sink half-performed cannot be concealed from you.*"

The Angel: "*I know.*"

The Newcomer: "*Oh, in such an hour was I born, and doubly fearful to me is the flaw in my heart. Must I drag my shame, Prince and Singer, all my days more bowed than my neighbour?*"

Silence: A Spiritual Journey Through PTSD

The Angel: "Without your wound where would your power be? It is your very sadness that makes your low voice tremble into the hearts of men. The very angels themselves cannot persuade the wretched and blundering children on earth as can one human being broken on the wheels of living. In Love's service only the wounded soldiers can serve. Draw back."

The doctor obeys and consequently gives up his opportunity for healing. A person who had been criticising the doctor for being there, is the one who is healed and is happy for a moment. But then he sees the doctor there and, remembering circumstances that await him at home, pleads with the doctor:

"But come with me first, an hour only, to my home. My son is lost in dark thoughts. I — I do not understand him, and only you have ever lifted his mood. Only an hour… my daughter, since her child has died, sits in the shadow. She will not listen to us but she will listen to you."

Broken on the wheels of living. In love's service, only wounded soldiers can serve. My pain was great, at times unbearable still. But I could not deny that when I saw people, I was able, more than ever before, to see the pain behind the smiling mask. And usually when I asked them how they were, I was right.

"Without your wound, where would your power be?" Was it true that my ability to see others in their pain, was due to the fact that I myself was wounded? My younger years, whilst not the most disastrous, had featured one incident in my teens which had left an open wound which I hadn't realised until a good decade later. I saw too that it had taken me into lengthy periods of depression from the age of about fifteen onwards. I didn't recognise it for what it was until my descent into PTSD and major depression, when I looked back on those dark episodes with one of those "Aha!" moments. I was now able to see them for what they were. For most of my life from the age of fifteen onwards, depressive episodes occurred every few months, triggered by goodness knows what because they were so long ago. They occurred with such frightening regularity that I thought that everyone was like that.

But in addition to these negatives, there was a positive. I felt I could see past the masks which people sometimes wear.

There is an activity that I get kids to participate in during drama lessons involving the development of subtext. In it, I will get them to say a single word, such as "Hi" in as many different contexts as possible. They were able to learn how to convey meaning with their bodies or with the tone of their voice.

It was quite disconcerting but without fail, when I spoke with people it was as if I could hear the words beneath the words, or see another face behind the mask. And I am convinced now that I look back that it was due to the woundedness of my teenage years.

There is a form of Japanese art called *wabi-sabi*. At its foundation it holds that brokenness contains beauty. This form of art can use different media such as stained glass, pottery and even just furniture but its focus is on how the imperfect, the broken, the asymmetrical is beautiful and suggests to us that nothing is ever perfect, everlasting or complete. Authenticity is lauded.

Looking for beauty in imperfection and pain goes against the grain of many societies however. Especially in our post-modern Western consumer driven part of the world where success, strength and perfection are nobility. However as has been demonstrated in recent times, all it takes is for one tiny virus to dismantle this belief, and reveal that behind the curtain, the Wizard is just a plain old man with a bunch of tricks.

Pain that is not transformed is transmitted. Pain that is not dealt with finds its expression in ugly ways: through depression, through domestic violence, eating disorders, suicide. And these effects are far reaching, as the proverbial ripple in a pond. Pain that is dealt with thoroughly can be transformed into ways beyond what we can imagine or dream.

As I look back on what happened to me that day, I could never have imagined what my life would be like almost a decade later. My calling became clearer as a result of that day and I am so much more fulfilled now than I ever was then. Back then I worked a job. Now I'm living a calling. I was wounded terribly that day, but because I dealt with those wounds in a thorough way, those wounds have helped in the healing of others. Our healed wounds cry out "hope" to others and declare that in weakness strength can be found. It is a message that a broken and bleeding world is crying out for.

Without our wounds, where would our power come from?

Life in the Laundromat

It was mid April and it had rained for two days on our little island paradise. It usually only rains for five minutes at a time where we live – something about a rain shadow. My dog, Maggie, ever the barometer, snuggled up close to me at every possible moment, a shadow of a more welcome kind.

In a burst of activity a day or two before the downpour, we had managed to put a few loads of washing on the line to hopefully dry in the mid Autumn sun. Autumn weather on the south coast is close to perfection: still, clear crisp days, with the occasional overnight shower. So we were confident that our washing would dry that day, or at the most the next.

And so on that next day, because it only ever rains for five minutes down here when the heavens opened up, I thought little of it and did not immediately race outside to bring the washing in. I was fully expecting the sun to be out shortly and I'd bring it in later.

But it rained all that day... and the next... and there was no sign of it letting up. My veggie patch was so grateful for it but we were running out of essential clothing. So I decided on that second day to take the washing from the line to the laundrette. It was truly soaked. The rain had even come from a different direction, so the protection usually afforded by the strategic position of our clothes line was non existent. I loaded up a basket and off I went.

Arriving at the laundrette, I loaded up the dryer, opened up my iPad and began reading a psych text, preparing for my next assignment. There was another guy there, about my age, wrestling with a washing machine's instructions and not winning. Eventually, he thought he may have figured out what was happening with the machine (he hadn't, as it turned out) and sat down next to me.

I continued to read for a little while but then I decided to be friendly and started to talk to him. Initially, I asked him if he lived in town, or if he was down on holidays. It was the school holidays. First term had just finished and even with the rain, there were quite a few unfamiliar faces in town. Our town was large enough to not bump into everyone all of the time but tourists always seemed to have a certain "look" about them which I had tried define but couldn't quite put my finger on. It was the relaxed-but-simultaneously-frazzled look of parents that often gave it away, I think.

It turned out that he was local, though. Well, only just local. He had moved down to our sleepy little town in January of that year. He had bought a houseboat and was moored at a marina nearby. I kept engaging him (turns out we shared first names) and discovered, to my amazement, that his present girlfriend now lived two streets over from where our family had moved from in Para Hills West seven years previously. Small world....

I asked what had led to him moving down. As he began speaking, I detected a tremor, both in voice and in his eyes. "This man is broken," I thought. He began to share about the past year and how he had been diagnosed with PTSD after an incident at a hotel where he had been working. He had been employed as a pokie machine attendant but he kept on being asked to intervene whenever altercations arose between patrons, or if people came in just to cause trouble. It was on one of the latter occasions, where a gang had come in, that his manager had asked him to "deal with it."

What I haven't revealed is that Andrew was a bikie. Though below average height, he was stocky, well muscled, with several earrings in his left ear, and am impressive sleeve of tattoos on his right arm. He had taken me through his sleeve, pointing out Ned Kelly, the Glenrowan pub famous from the days of Kelly, a few skulls and other features meaningful to his life.

Life in the Laundromat

A bikie. Tough. Uncompromising. He had shared with me several accounts of chopping ears off of people who had crossed him, leading to his unlikely nickname – Chopper. I shifted uncomfortably in my seat and wondered to myself whether the washing was dry enough yet.

But here he was now, noticeably softer, brokenness evident in his voice. He shared how that one of the hotel altercations had had a profound effect on his life, after lies had been spoken about his actions in the incident in the aftermath. He had suffered nightmares, constant flashbacks and could not cope living as close as he did to this pub. He was offered a payout and with it he took the opportunity to move down to the south coast, bought the houseboat and now just wanted to be left alone so that he could fish.

As he spoke, I felt an incredible affinity with him. He spoke freely of his pain that came out of the event. I haven't spoken of it in detail here but I could easily see how it would have broken even someone seemingly as tough and hard as he. Eventually after he had finished, I shared my story. Two people from such diverse backgrounds and experiences. We couldn't be more different. Apart from our names and the geographical proximity of our former locations we were at opposite ends of a few different spectrums. But we had both experienced pain. We had been drawn into each other's stories and in sharing with each other, our pain had been lessened to a degree.

Well, possibly not lessened. Perhaps lightened is a more appropriate word. Shared.

One of my favourite scenes from the LOTR movies occurs near the end of *The Return of the King*. Frodo has carried the ever increasing burden of the ring to the very slopes of Mt Doom. The end is in sight. But the sheer weight of the ring; of the burden that he alone must carry becomes too much now that he is so close to achieving his quest. Seeing the effect of the ring on his dear friend, Samwise Gamgee, knows that he cannot take the ring from Frodo and carry it himself, so instead he tries to focus

Frodo on something more familiar and pleasant. When that doesn't work, he utters some powerful words.

He asks Frodo if he remembers the Shire. He reminds him that it will soon be spring again and all that entails in the Shire: that the orchards will be blossoming again and that the summer barley will be sown and the first of the strawberries will have arrived. Sam asks Frodo if he can recall the taste of strawberries.

In the relentless fog caused by the weight of the Ring, Frodo says that he can't recall any of these things. He confesses to Sam that he feels alone, naked, exposed, with nothing protecting him from the fire of Mordor.

With that, Sam who himself had come to a low place, exclaims, "I can't carry it for you. But I can carry you." And with those words, Samwise takes Frodo onto his shoulders and carries him up the mountain. He couldn't take Frodo's pain but he could carry him in his pain in order to lighten the load.

As we shared our familiar journeys that rainy day in the laundrette, our first name was not all that we had in common. As Andrew spoke of his pain and as I listened without judgement and uttered words in reply which demonstrated that I "heard" him – and that he had been seen, I saw the pain in his eyes decrease for a time. I felt my burden lighten too.

We may not be able to take on another's pain but we can carry them for a time. Until it's our turn to be carried for a while.

Lesson from the Road #2

Sometimes when you're running
You find yourself running into a gale force wind.
Every step that you take
Seems to get you nowhere,
Even though you are trying harder than you normally do.

You try and you try
And even though you think
You have no strength to combat the gale,
You do somehow reach the halfway mark
And turn for home.

And when you do,
You find that without the wind in your face,
You do indeed have energy
And more than you thought.

And you find that
The constant buffeting of the gale
Has made you strong

And sometimes
This doesn't just apply to running

Back to Earth

I could have strangled my psychiatrist today – preferably with a skipping rope!

I had felt so much better in the previous few weeks. I wasn't sleeping the whole day away. I was feeling as if I was being productive, both at home and at the school where I had been placed to complete "project work." My mood was so much better. I was even cracking really bad jokes again. So I went along to my session, feeling really good about myself.

We went through the standard process: what's new, how has your mood been, how is your eating/sleeping etc etc. I answered all of these confidently and I guess maybe a little smugly. I felt so on top of things.

I did describe one moment at school, where a boy had run away from his class and I had helped to look for him. I shared about how the boy was found at the playground and that I had a feeling that's where he may have been. But I was reticent to approach it. I hadn't been to a playground since the incident and in no way wanted to broach that potential trigger at such a moment.

The psychiatrist listened to me and then, laughingly, told me an account of a colleague who had suffered a panic attack at his work and so, in order to recover from the experience, he left the building and went for a walk in a park. After some time walking, he came across a man hanging from a tree. He was near death and the colleague had to get him down. My psychiatrist told me this story with a laugh and a twinkle in his eye.

But my mood changed in an instant. I averted my eyes and my body started to shake. My confidence, which had seemed at a year long high, shattered into a million pieces, unable to be glued back together again with any sense of certainty that the right pieces were in the right place.

He looked at me and I finally met his gaze and held it for a moment. He began to speak.

Back to Earth

"You see? There are triggers all around you and despite the way you were feeling when you came in, can you see that the trauma is still there, not far from the surface at all?"

Brought back to earth in an instant... All that I felt I had been building came crashing down... I stared at the broken pieces lying on the ground and wondered how long it would take to build it all up again. I felt so tired again.

dɪˈprɛʃ(ə)n/

Depression.

One word. So many nuances.

I love words. I love trying to paint pictures with words, whether that be in my report writing in order to bring some light and shade to what can be very dry, in my creative writing, or in my songwriting, to try to get close to the music that I hear in my head most of the day. Lately, in my work with disability and counselling, it seems to be zeroing in on the best words to describe what a person is working through in their daily battles.

This word 'depression.' I venture to say that when this word is spoken today it forms a picture in a person's mind that would likely centre on the notion of mental health. Depression – that psychosocial illness causing feelings of sadness, lethargy, fatigue, lack of appetite and loss of interest in activities that make a person come alive. At its worst, it can make a person feel that life is not worth living, and for a Christian, for someone who believes that the Maker of heaven and earth, of all that is, seen and unseen, it can be even more debilitating. I haven't been in that place where I felt that life was no longer worth living but I have been in that dark, airless room where I couldn't understand how the illness known as depression had such a hold on me, despite what I believed about the fullness of Christ, and how He filled me in every way. Why was it that I was constantly brought down by this "thing", if the power that God the Father exerted in raising Christ from the dead and seated Him at His right hand, far above every other power in all of Creation, was at work in me, as Paul says in Ephesians 1?

In my effort to understand how it was that I wasn't being the overcoming Christian I desired and believed I could and should be, I began to see that I needed to have a better understanding of my adversary. Know your enemy, right? And for me to know my enemy, I saw that I needed to use my interest in words to gain understanding. For my

/dɪˈprɛʃ(ə)n/

whole life, ever since I can remember, I've been one who wanted to understand pain; I saw the value and necessity of examining the items in the backpack I was carrying so that I could understand what was weighing me down. The clinical definition of depression for me, a poet, was just that – too clinical. It seemed to me the clinical descriptions didn't give depression a body. They are descriptive, yes, but they don't give you a full picture of the beast. They simplify it down to single words. And depression is anything but simple.

So I began to explore the other non-psychosocial meanings of this one word 'depression' in order to gain further insight.

Depression can be seen as a verb as well as a noun. When it used as a verb, it can be used, though not often, to describe the action where someone lowers something into a hole. So often in the dead of depression, yes I could relate to that sensation of being lowered, powerless, into a hole. I have spoken of it elsewhere here but I don't think I have described it adequately enough. Depression is being lowered down into a well against your will. As you are being lowered, and the bucket descends into progressively darker and danker air, you have no clue as to what lies beneath. Water? Will I drown? Snakes? I've seen those *Indiana Jones* movies. I hate snakes too. And, is there an end to this descent or will I just be lowered deeper and deeper indefinitely? Will I ever bottom out? Will it ever end?

That uncertainty creates both a panic and a feeling of utter helplessness. Your life is out of your control. Alone in the bucket, you are a slave to whomever or whatever is lowering the bucket into the depths. I've been in that sunken place.

When it is used as a verb, 'depression' can also be used to describe pressing something down. Every time I thought that I was rising, vivid video replays in my head, accusing thoughts and more, pressed firmly on my head, forcing me back down to where I had been previously. It was a dead weight, against which I had no strength to push back against.

Silence: A Spiritual Journey Through PTSD

'Depression' can have a meteorological use as well. When it is used in this way, it designates a region that has a lower atmospheric pressure when compared to other regions adjacent to it. It can especially be used to describe a cyclonic weather system. In my world of low atmospheric pressure, it seemed that wherever I went, I created a gloom; a long, damp, soaking rain in a land which craved sunshine. I don't know if that's true but it's the way I felt and so for a long time at family gatherings, or when I was with acquaintances, I sat quietly, hoping that attention wouldn't be drawn to the trough of low pressure that I had brought with me. I felt like I had a constant cloud over my head.

As this particular depressive episode descended into chronic depression and continued for weeks, then months, and then years, I came to see that periodic depression was something that had been a pattern throughout most of my life. I could identify an incident way back in my teenage years where this pattern had been set into motion and I could see the rising and falling of my mood from that moment, on through my teens unchecked, into my twenties and thirties, through marriage and the beginnings of parenthood, and into my forties. A constant cloud over my head. I could feel it there, always just above and behind me. It seemed as if I could just reach up with my hands, I could wave it away.

Depression is a cyclone. Destructive, unpredictable, constantly on the move, forming and reforming, changing direction, creating havoc and despair in the lives of all who are in its path. A wrecker of homes. You see, it's not just the sufferer of depression who suffers. Those in the immediate path of the cyclone suffer deeply, often silently. And unlike a meteorological cyclone, sometimes they don't even know that they are affected by it, until one day they look around at the remains of their once strong house, their family life and see nothing but ruin, destruction. I have no idea of the pain and suffering I caused my family during those two years of PTSD but more so, through the years before that, where I see now that I was a phantom in their lives. I desperately wanted to be a good *dɪˈprɛʃ(ə)n/*

dad but the tropical low rained on that desire. And it seemed it was always wet season.

Depression is all of these things. But even after all of these descriptions, both clinical and metaphorical, it is so much more. We are complex, fearfully and wonderfully made creatures, a mix of biology, psychology and sociology, and even then, so much more. To clinically know depression doesn't mean that you understand completely someone who is experiencing it. And to know someone who is experiencing depression is not to know depression completely.

Interlude 5

I wonder what "the day" will look like
I wonder if I will be aware of its arrival
Or if it will walk in quietly, unannounced
And I'll just know
That it's over
That I've come through the storm
And have found safe harbour

Maybe it will be like the time
When I was driving
And I saw a rainbow up ahead
And, as I watched it
As I drove
It drew closer and closer
Brilliant, vivid in its colours
And though I knew
That there would be no pot of gold
At the end of it
It filled me with a sense of anticipation anyway

I continued to draw close to it
As I made my way up the winding incline
Between Goolwa and Mt. Compass
And, as I broke through to open country
There it was
In a cow paddock
In all its glory
Fully formed
ROYGBIV

Interlude 5

For all the world to see
Well, anyone on that road anyway

And then it was close enough
That if I chose to stop at that moment-
Instead of racing to whatever mental health appointment
I was supposed to be at
I felt that I could reach out and touch it
A sign of promise
Ready to be taken hold of

But I drove on
And suddenly
It was behind me
Just like that
A vision that soon disappeared
From the rear vision mirror

Maybe "the day"
Will be just like that
Visible up ahead
Though the road is steep and winding
Vivid
Glorious
Full of promise
So close I can reach out and touch it

But then
Just like that
In a moment
Behind me

Without fanfare and fuss
As I travel on
Through open country

Embrace the Silence

Tonight, instead of the beach, I went to the river to run along the path alongside it. It is one of my favourite routes, especially when the day is still and cool. Houses line one side of Liverpool Rd but they are set well back and don't crowd the area at all, and the other side gives a mostly clear view of the river. I enjoy this run because it obviously follows the river and I love watching the bird life: pelicans, ibis, pesky plovers, and water hens all doing their stuff. Thankfully the plovers are mostly well behaved. I think they tend to nest in more remote locations.

Anyway, after my run, it was dusk. The first day of winter, it was a cool, crisp and totally still evening. To cool down, I walked around for a while, rehydrating as I went. The place where I usually park has a boat ramp and a cute little jetty next to it, and I decided to walk out on to the jetty and stretch.

As I stretched weary muscles, I was struck by something.

The silence.

No wind. Not a sound from birds who had packed up for the day while I was running and were now heading home for the night. No traffic, from either the road or the river. Not a single person out for their evening walk. Dusk had come and every created thing had gone home it seemed. Except for me. I was alone.

Alone in the silence. I stood there in awe and listened. I drank it in. I was in the middle of exam preparation and the day had not been as productive as I had hoped. As I stood in the silence and listened, I strained my ears, hoping to hear in that silence the things I needed to hear.

There is an ancient account about the Jewish prophet Elijah. He has just had a showdown with Ahab (not the sea captain but the king). During this showdown, he has challenged the 450 prophets of Baal to a test. They are to choose two bulls to sacrifice: one to Baal and one to Elijah's god, Jehovah. Both Elijah and the prophets are to prepare their prospective bulls for sacrifice. They are to both place the bulls on their respective fireplaces but then wait and see which god burns the sacrifices. Neither Elijah nor the prophets of Baal are to ignite their sacrifice. That is the job of their chosen god. They are both to pray and whichever god answers by burning up the sacrifice, he is God.

So Elijah lets the prophets of Baal go first. Very decent of him. They call on the name of their god from morning till noon. At noon Elijah starts goading them, urging them to call out with louder voices.

"Perhaps your god is asleep."

"He could be deep in thought."

"Maybe he's on the toilet."

And the prophets of Baal became more frenzied in their appeals to Baal, shouting louder and when that fails, they start to slash their wrists with swords. Of course, all of this was to no avail. They fall exhausted to the ground and turn their attention to Elijah's sacrifice. It was his god's turn.

Elijah prepares his sacrifice but then asks the people to pour water over the sacrifice. Not satisfied, he asks them to pour even more water over it and asks again a third time. Finally, Elijah steps forward and prays in a loud voice asking his god to answer his prayer. Of course, fire falls from heaven, and burns up the sacrifice, along with the wood, the stones and the soil. It dries up the water in the trench that had been dug around the sacrifice. The people who had gathered fall prostrate on the ground in terror and Elijah orders the arrest of the prophets of Baal, who are summarily slaughtered.

Embrace the Silence

You would think after this episode that Elijah would be on top of the world. But no. Jezebel, King Ahab's wife hears of Elijah's victory and threatens his life. Surprisingly, Elijah runs for his life, and after a series of days in the wilderness, ends up in a cave, depressed, wanting to die. He spends the night there and the next day God comes to him and asks what he's doing there. Elijah tells God all that has happened and ends up by saying that he's the only faithful person left.

He is alone. Alone in the silence.

God tells him to go outside the cave because He is about to pass by.

A powerful wind comes, tears at the mountains and shatters rocks. But the account says that God was not in the wind. Nor was He in the earthquake that followed, or the fire after that.

A silence follows.

And in that silence, Elijah hears a gentle whisper. It is the voice of God and in that gentle whisper, Elijah is given comfort and direction for a positive future.

As I stood in my silence at the end of my run, my thoughts turned to the day when I had saved a boy's life. That day, I had achieved a great victory. That day, I expected to find myself on top of the world. Nothing could defeat me.

But that wasn't how it turned out for me. Instead I found myself in a cave. Alone. Defeated. Despairing for the future. In silence.

The cyclonic winds, the earthquake, and the fire of PTSD and depression and the rehabilitation process came, and were shaking me to the core and in the advice that I was being given, I was finding no comfort. It was only in the silence, in the cave, or more for my story, on my windswept, deserted beach and here by the river that I felt I might find answers. But the answers that came and even more to the point, the questions that preceded them, were not always pleasant. Rarely so. But I somehow knew, as I ran my windswept beach, that it was in the silence that I, as with Elijah, would find my answers. Hope and direction for a positive future.

The novel, *The Chosen*, by Chaim Potok details the friendship between two Jewish boys from post World War 2 Brooklyn and tensions that arise as their ancient culture collides with the modern world. One of the boys, Reuven is the son of an Orthodox Jew and the other Danny, the son of Reb, the head of a Hasidic dynasty. Danny's father has raised him in silence, having little conversation with him. Late in the novel, after the boys have grown up, grown apart and then reconciled, Reb asks Reuven over one night and Reuven realises that he is being used by Reb to speak indirectly into Danny's life to explain his actions. Reb explains about his silence.

He explains to Danny through his words to Reuven that even in the silence, you can listen, and in that silence, you can listen and learn from silence's unique qualities and dimensions. Silence is not just silence. Reb confesses to Reuven that sometimes he can hear the silence talking to him and within its beautiful complexity, sometimes he can hear it not only talking but crying. And in that crying Reb says that he can hear the pain of the world. Voices crying out in a silence that cannot be heard unless you commit to listen, despite the fact that you leave yourself open to taking on that very pain. In the listening there is pain; it is a given. But despite this, Reb said he cannot help but listen.

Oh, how that resonated within me, as I thought back to the silences that I was experiencing. I had so many questions. Questions about depression, about PTSD, about why I was struggling to overcome it, about why Azim and others I had come across in my journey, like Robert, would ever come to a point where ending their own life was logical and preferable. And as I shouted my questions to the silence, there was no reply. It didn't talk but paradoxically, I sometimes heard it cry and in that cry I heard not only my pain but the pain of others who also screamed out to the silence. And yes, it hurt to listen but I knew I had to.

I was drawn to the silence. I found it somehow mystical, and again, paradoxical. It was beautiful, yet terrible. It was simple but complex, passive but active. It was both a lamb and a lion. It was comfort but it tore me apart. It was a thousand contradictions but completely integrated. I sat in that silence. I ran in the silence. That night after my run, I waited in awe in that silence. I both hated and loved the silence.

In time, I hoped I would be able to embrace the silence.

The Doctor

Crash. Just like that. All the hard work. Gone. After a year of scrambling to try and find hand and footholds in the well worn sides of the well, I found myself in a heap at the bottom instead.

I had been required, as part of the work rehab process to attend an assessment to be conducted by an "independent" psychiatrist. This was so that my employer could ascertain whether or not I was fit enough to return to work. Apparently, it was standard practice. A year had passed since I had left work and they wanted to know if I was better after all of their hard work rehabilitating me.

I'm so sorry. On rereading, that last paragraph sounds oh, so cynical. Again my apologies. I really don't know what came over me. Obviously I am profoundly thankful for all that was done for me in my rehab process....

Whoops. Again, sorry.

After an hour and a half drive, I arrived at my appointment early but could only find a parking place for one hour, and the meeting was supposed to go for an hour and a half. After I was ushered into the meeting, I explained my parking predicament. The psychiatrist, a female and somewhat younger than me (I later found out from my psychiatrist that she had been practising psychiatry for six months. Imagine potentially placing someone's future in one so young), said that we should start and review the parking situation closer to when the hour was up. I was happy with that.

All the "assessment" involved was me re-telling the incident for the umpteenth time. By this time, I was prepared for such occasions. Some months before, I had begun to compile detailed notes on the events surrounding that day. I wanted to make sure that if I was ever asked about it again (and again and again) I would not miss anything important. So, during this assessment, as I recounted the incident (again), I constantly referred to my iPad notes to ensure that I was accurate in my recount.

The problem I was having at that stage was that my expressive language was cumbersome. I found it so hard to string together anything approaching what I considered to be coherent sentences. I stumbled in the dark from one word, or, on a good day, one phrase to the next, not really sure where I had come from and stretching out my arms in front of me as I tentatively took each step, so that I would not bump into any unseen obstacles.

And so, iPad in hand, I recounted the day. The doctor listened and took notes, and then asked a few questions. She then said she was sorry for what I had been through and thanked me for coming. I looked at my iPad: I still had ten minutes before my parking spot expired. I asked if I should move my car and the psychologist said "No" and that the assessment was complete. Confused and rather perturbed I left the room and started the hour and a half drive back home. I estimated that the supposed ninety minute assessment had lasted forty-five minutes at the most.

The crash came a few weeks later when, in an appointment with my regular psychiatrist, he handed me a copy of the resulting report to peruse and make comments on. Halfway down the second page, a siren started sounding off in my head.

"I met with the client for a total of 1 hour and 30 minutes."
    What?!

What followed was a litany of misquotes, misrepresentations and misinterpretations, and recommendations based on those misunderstandings. If it had not be so negligent, it would have been laughable.

I didn't laugh. The black cloud which, through much beach running, dog hugging, gardening and rest had receded to a degree, returned suddenly as a full force storm front. Once again, I was helpless in the maelstrom.

I could not believe what I was reading.

According to her account, instead of me holding on to the feet of a boy to prevent the final stages of him hanging himself from some cricket nets, history was rewritten to become "The boy eventually lowered himself down the cricket nets and started to climb down. The client grabbed hold of the boy's feet in order to support him in the process of climbing down."

All that I had been through that day with Azim was immediately invalidated. What was my problem? After all, according to her, all I had done was help a distressed boy climb back down to the ground. How could something like that lead to PTSD and major depression. Wasn't I overreacting? Or worse, faking? And the account was all there in official black and white.

This misrepresentation wasn't the only one: it went on for page after page but this was the one which stood out because misunderstanding the actual event meant that the entire assessment was skewed entirely to the "not critical" end of the scale.

A few others...

"I met with the client for a total of one hour and thirty minutes."
    Yeah, right.

"The client explained to me that although he was based at that school, he could move around to different schools because he was a relief teacher."

The Doctor

I had actually said that, as a relief teacher I had no base and that this was why I felt I was struggling to regain health. With no base, no community, I had no one beside me, supporting me in my recovery and nowhere to look forward to return to. There was no goal, and without having a perceivable goal, people perish.

Apparently I had a "Diploma of Training" not a Diploma of Teaching.

"He has also worked with Year 12 Special Ed students."
Well actually, I had run Special Ed departments for twelve years.

"He referred to his iPad and essentially read what was recorded on there."
Well, you know, sometimes it's important to have your facts straight. As I said, at that stage, I couldn't string a sentence together. I needed something to support me, and my iPad was it.

"The boy tried tying the skipping rope to the top railing of the cricket nets."
No, the boy DID tie the rope to the railing. Not just one time but many times. I told you that!

"The boy ran to the other side of the cricket nets and tied the skipping rope into a part of it."
Well, no. He was still on top of the nets, not on the ground as your sentence implies. He scrambled over to the other side, and retied the rope to the top railing. I ran around with the chair to where he was, climbed it and cut the rope again, trying to get as close to Azim as possible, so that the length of rope would shorten at a quicker rate. He repeated the process of scrambling and retying a number of times (perhaps five in total?) and eventually the rope was too short for him to tie it to anything. When he realised this, he began to throw asphalt and rocks at me and

another male teacher who had arrived by that time. I was very clear about this.

"The client reported that he has now returned to school in an administrative role."

I had absolutely no idea where this one came from. I had not returned to any school in any capacity. There were plans for me to return to a school in some sort of research role but this had not eventuated at that stage because my health was so poor.

"He will continue with this work for the next three weeks until the term finishes."

Well, since I wasn't working anywhere, I don't know how I could have continued it for another three weeks. Some of the things that I read were unfathomable and I had no clue how she had come up with this from what I had said.

"He has convinced himself that he can never return to teaching…"

This one really hurt. I couldn't understand how a professional could come up with such a judgemental view after less than an hour. Yes, at the time I was incredibly hesitant to return to teaching because of my state of health. Behaviour management, hours and hours of planning, staff meetings, reports, excursions, parent teacher interviews, curriculum development, professional development, to name a few, as well as the actual act of teaching, would have placed a stress on me that would have been of further detriment to my health. But at that stage I had not "convinced" myself that I could never return. I had been a teacher for twenty five years and it was not something that one throws away when things get hard. I had been a teacher who, over those twenty five years, had helped many children deal with hurts, strengthened weakness, and find their place and their giftings. That was not something that a person just suddenly throws away.

The Doctor

I found errors in almost every paragraph. In the comfy chair, in the relative safety of the psychiatrist's office, I felt heavy. Exhausted. Down the bottom of the deep, dark hole again, knowing that the scramble out had to start all over again.

The rehab process had claimed me again. It was proving to be more damaging than the initial incident had been. It seemed to me that it was more about jumping through the recommended appointment hoops and having the right medical forms signed than it was about rest and recovery. I was driving an exorbitant distance to the psychiatrist recommended to me by my GP. In all, it was a two and a half hour round trip, so a one hour appointment became an entire day away from the solitude and safety of home.

After appointments, I often arrived home totally spent, seemingly further away from recovery than I had been at the start of the day. All I could do after appointments, as with any appointment that I attended, whether it be psychiatrist, psychologist or just my doctor, was walk through the door, grab hold of Maggie, my dog and disappear into the bedroom for the rest of the day.

This day was no different in that regard. I arrived home, made a beeline to Maggie, scooped her in my arms and headed off to bed. I lay there, mortified, replaying the words, phrases and sentences in my head over and over. It was Depression 201: I had made it through the initial phase with flying colours (that is, I was still well and truly depressed and suffering PTSD). But this, this next phase, stirred everything up all over again.

The voices that screamed at me increased in volume and started to have an accusing tone to them, thanks to the invalidation in the report provided by the good doctor.

"You've been imagining what happened that day."

"It really wasn't as bad as you made it out to be."

"You're milking this for all it's worth."

"Just suck it in, get up and get moving. Enough."

"She's right. You have convinced yourself you can never return to teaching. You're using this as an excuse."

I found out later on that this psychiatrist, fresh out of university, had been flown in from Sydney for the day, obviously at great expense. It was bemusing to me that, if someone was to be flown all that way, why they couldn't at least show adequate listening skills. I mean, that's their job isn't it?

This event happened in April 2013: a year out from the original incident. From where I sat – no, lay – in my dark, curtained bedroom, I was further away from recovery than I had ever been. All the appointments that I was required to attend were not seeming to do anything to help me to recover. In fact, they seemed to be making things worse. Maggie was proving to be better therapy for me than anything a human was attempting to provide. Maggie, faithful, non judgemental, patient (apart from meal times) and always ready to spend time by my side in silence.

Validation

It hit me again today, from out of the blue. I was listening to the radio on the way to my workcover placement of an account by a boy who had been wrongly accused of downloading porn to his school's computers. The boy was actually innocent: It seemed that a teacher had been doing it using the boy's login.

I listened to the boy, as I sat there in the staff car park, horrified at his story. All he wanted was an apology, an acknowledgement or affirmation from the education department that he was innocent but instead of this he had been offered a sum of money as compensation. A nice thought I guess but it wasn't what the boy wanted or needed in order to move on. All he wanted was someone to say sorry.

As I listened, I was filled with an intense sadness. I realised that with me and my experience, no one had ever said thank you to me. Not Azim's mother or family – not that I ever met them, not his teacher, not any staff member, certainly not the principal and definitely none of the powers-that-be in the department. Quite the opposite actually, in the latter case.

All I had received from them was the opportunity to view a psychologist's report about Azim, completed after the incident. In it the psychologist stated that Azim was never going to commit suicide but that he was simply reenacting a "game" that he had seen his mother play out, back in Sudan. That's right, he was just playing. When he was lowering himself over the edge of the cricket nets with a noose around his neck, he was only playing a game. Once he was lowered over the cricket nets, no doubt the game would be over. No winners.

I had expended all my physical and emotional energy just to stop, not an attempt to end a life, but someone playing a game.

Yeah, right …

Validation has a number of meanings but one of them involves the recognition or affirmation of the feelings or opinions of someone else. It's about saying, "Yes" to them, even if you don't necessarily agree or understand completely. It's about withholding judgement. It's about abrogating any power that you may have over them, due to your position of authority or experience. In short, it's about grace.

The first rule of improvisation in drama is that you have to say, "Yes" to whatever the other actors on stage say or do. You have to accept their offers. It is the first improvisation skill taught and it is a hard one to master. Furthermore, you don't just have to say "Yes" to others, you have to say "Yes and…" In other words, you have to take what the other person says, accept it and then add to what the other person originally said. You give it further meaning, you extend and develop their idea, you explore it. In this way, a scene can develop. Saying "No" blocks the scene, making it difficult for a story to unfold.

Some students that I introduce this concept to really struggle with the whole having-to-agree-with-the-other-person idea, and while they get to the point of being able to say "Yes" to the other person, instead of saying, "Yes and …", they will say "Yes but …" This is the same as saying, "No."

Saying, "Yes and…" to the other person validates the offer of the original actor, adds further ideas, emotions or information, sets creativity free and enables the scene to develop.

My offer was that I had saved a boy's life. Other actors on the stage that day agreed with me. Jane – the SSO on her last day there, one of the male teachers who said to me that it was the worst thing he had seen in his thirty years of teaching. But the education department, the Workcover system were not following the rules of the stage. They were either saying, "No" or "Yes but…" to my offer, thus blocking my original offer, which had the effect of failing to allow the scene, that is, my recovery, to develop.

Validation

Where was the validation from the people that held top status in the scene? Many people who hadn't been there on that day, or who were removed from the education system had told me that I was a hero that day. I appreciated their words. But I needed something more. I needed a thank you from my superiors. A gracious thankful response from the powers that be. An acknowledgement that what I had done was important; that I had, in fact, intervened after their well-planned structures had failed that day and not only saved a life but saved them from severe repercussions.

But no, there had been none. Just silence – as if any acknowledgement on their behalf that this event was what it was, would somehow been a terrible admission of guilt. That they would somehow been liable. I certainly didn't feel this way.

How could anyone possibly justify behaving in such a manner? I would never dream of behaving that way. My immediate response would be sincere, extreme gratitude, along with a concern that all parties involved were safe and well.

I was just thankful that I had listened to a still, small voice saying, "Follow him". I was thankful, I really was, that I had said, "Yes, and…" to the offer from that still, small voice and so allowed that scene to unfold to its completion.

God forbid, what if I had said, "No?"

Lessons from the Beach #1

Sometimes when you're running
Along your beach of faith
The soft sand
Difficult as it already is
Seems to be quicksand
The tide is on the turn
And is gradually receding
But still at times
It forces you higher up the beach
Towards the dreaded sandhills

And every step
Feels as if the sand
Is going up to your knees
And every step
Feels as if it's your last

And you look in desperation
At the waves still crashing
So close to your feet
And you tire inside
Because you long
For firm footing

But you persevere
Because you have a goal to achieve
And you won't be beaten
By something as simple as soft sand

Lessons from the Beach #1

And then you reach halfway
And turn for home
And hunt for your footprints
And realise
That the tide has now turned
And your outbound trail
Is higher up the beach
In the soft sand of the past
But now because time has passed
You are on more stable ground

And so you find firmer footing
And the long run becomes easier
And, wonder of wonders
Enjoyable
Even though, every now and then
The tide catches you by surprise
And pushes you back
Higher up the beach
Into the soft sand again

But you know
That it's only for a short time
Because the tide has turned
And you'll be able to return
To the firm sand again

And you find
That the longer you persevere
In the soft sand
That you become

More confident and strong
Because of the time spent
Higher up the beach

And sometimes
This doesn't just apply to running

Treasures in Darkness

Apparently
There are treasures to be found
In darkness …

I haven't found this to be so
Yet …
Though I keep staggering
Uncertainly
Hesitantly
Hands outstretched
In front of me
Searching
I am still to uncover
Any pearl of great price …

But how will I know?
How am I to say
What is treasure
And what is of no use?

Nothing is wasted
I believe this to be true
And so, if nothing is wasted,
If everything that I encounter
Can be picked up
Turned over in my fumbling hands
And examined closely
Then all is treasure

So in darkness
As in light
All is treasure

The Silence of God

In the beginning, there was silence. Before God spoke and created all we see, the author of Genesis describes a formless void over which the Spirit of God hovered. Before that first word, the Spirit did not speak; the Spirit was silent. The Spirit of God had never uttered a Word: a silent Presence hovering over a silent emptiness.

But silence isn't a passive thing. It's active waiting. It's full of expectation. It's like children holding their breath on Christmas Eve, going to sleep with the knowledge that something special is about to happen.

And so, at the beginning of everything, we have a formless void. The Spirit of God hovers silently over it, waiting for the right moment to speak the first Word. Then, with that Word, everything we see (though not necessarily in its final form) comes into being. Just think about it: Nothing… nothing… nothing… nothing… God speaks… everything. All of a sudden the void makes sense, as what previously had been chaotic and formless, comes together when God breaks His silence and speaks His first Word.

There was also a time when Heaven fell silent. The book of Revelation says that there was silence in Heaven for half an hour. There are so many views on how to interpret the Book of Revelation. Some say that the events described in the book had already occurred some time between the birth of the church and the time the author wrote the letter. A second view sees the book of Revelation not as describing any actual events in particular but as a picture of the ongoing struggle between good and evil. Other lenses for interpretation see the book of Revelation as pointing to future events, that is, the end times, when Christ returns.

I kind of like the interpretive method which views Revelation through a "this is describing a worship service" lens. In Revelation, God is worshipped in response to His creative works, the redemption provided through Christ's sacrifice, for the coming marriage between Jesus and the church, and worship of all of this is expressed through praise, thanksgiving, song, prayer, offerings and silence.

Yes, worship in Revelation is expressed in silence. Just like Elijah in the cave, Job in ashes and Joseph in the dungeon.

Romans 12:1-2 encourages believers to view their lives as an act of worship. Everything we do, everything we say, all is done as an act of worship. Washing the dishes, hanging out the washing, it's all worship. An act where we give God a sacrifice of thanksgiving.

So, if life is viewed as an act of worship, then where does the silence described in the worship service that is the book of Revelation come into it?

I have come to wonder if silence is that moment where we see that everything we are, everything we have, all of our steps, are all due to the grace of God and all that we can do is bow down with our faces to the ground in acknowledgement of that, and wait for His answer. We lay there, waiting facedown in the dust, for Him, in His time, to raise us up. Silence becomes a worshipful act of faith.

There was another time of silence. It occurred on a day unlike any other. A stand-alone day.

It was the day God the Father fell silent. Despite the cries of His Son, bruised and bleeding, beaten and torn, languishing in anguish on the cross, naked for all the world to see, God stays silent. Despite the pleading of His Son, asking Him why He was being forgotten, God the Father does not utter a word.

"Why have You forsaken Me? Why, in my hour of greatest need, are You not here?"

But there was silence in Heaven. No answer from the Father for the question tormenting the Son.

Why was heaven so silent? Why was there seemingly no answer when something so horrible was occurring?

The Silence of God

This was the same question that taunted me for two years in my pain. Why?

But in the silence on that greatest of days, God was speaking. Without words, He was speaking His final Word. In the silence of Jesus' death, He was saying that this event was the answer to all of our questions about suffering and evil. This profound mystery of God coming to this world and inhabiting skin and dying was the answer to all of the horrible silences of our lives.

It is finished. It is over. There is no more. There is nothing, no evil, no pain, no noise to get in the way, no confusing events without an answer. There is nothing that can ever bring you to the point of confusion ever again. There is only this moment with a man hanging on a cross, dying for all those moments when we crave silence from all the confusion and despair from life.

So, for me in my journey through PTSD, there came a moment where I too had to fall silent in worship and lie prostrate in the empty void that I felt I had been pulled into, and wait patiently for the Spirit of God, always hovering over and within me, often in silence, to speak the Word that would bring about a new creation out of the chaos within me. I had to stop pounding the beach, kilometre after kilometre, searching the sand and the wind and the waves for answers and accept that the day with Azim and the resulting PTSD somehow had to fit into my life of worship, even if it meant it was the time when I was to fall silent for half an hour, waiting in expectation for the Spirit to speak.

We see things, we judge things, we experience things and try to understand them and give them meaning from within the confines of the construct of time. But while God stepped into time and dwelt with us in Jesus, He exists apart from time. He sees all events, all things clearly, not through a dark glass, as we do when we try to understand the sometimes incomprehensible through the lens of time.

And so, in the end, I, a drama teacher, had to obey the first rule of improvisation: to say, "Yes" to those moments with Azim and the years of PTSD and all their chaos and turmoil. I had been saying, "No…" or "Yes but…" for two years, to all that I was experiencing and because of this, the scene was not able to be developed and move to resolution. All that saying no was doing was leading me to criticise, judge and analyse everything that was happening, instead of leaning back in the strong arms of God, and saying, "Yes and, … Lord Your will be done" and let Him bring the scene to its resolution.

I had to believe that God would, in His time, make all things new in me; that He would somehow make sense of the seemingly shapeless void of the madness that I was experiencing, and form something new, something beautiful, something unexpected from it. Indeed, my painful, messy prayer through all of 2013 and into 2014 was simply, "God, do something unexpected."

He did.

Silence

Music has been a constant companion since my very early years. When I was eight, I began my musical journey by taking up the viola. Yes, I know. Hold the viola jokes please because I've heard them all.

Definition of perfect pitch? Yes, a viola into a lake....

I learnt viola till I was 14 but then as peer pressure would have it, I was too embarrassed to let it be known that I played a STRINGED instrument, let alone the viola. So I then took up the clarinet. A great choice for looking cool. My wonderful hyper-extensive fingers didn't enjoy clarinet though, so for some reason a music teacher suggested saxophone. I was hooked and went on to study it at university level for a few years. Down the track as I commenced my teaching career, I taught myself guitar. Very simple style but effective for working with kids.

Singing was also a love. I was briefly involved in a jazz choir at university and we toured at the end of each year. I loved performing. Me, an introverted shy person, who didn't speak until he was in Year 4 at school, performing. I remember so clearly the day when at university (when I describe it as university, just picture a scene from the old TV series *Fame* and that would be it), it was the day for us to be told whether we were soprano, alto, tenor, or bass, and that would require us to sing solo in front of everyone else. I sat there terrified through the first day, and then the next, until my turn came. The piano started playing, I opened my mouth to sing for the first time on my own, hoping that something, anything would emanate from my mouth.

I sang. I can't remember what I had to sing but when I was done, there was silence in the room for an uncomfortable amount of time for me, before the lecturer said, "Yes, well, that's a wonderfully light tenor voice. Thank you."

And that was it. What did that mean? I had no idea and spent the next thirty years or so wondering if I did sound okay, until I reached a point where I just didn't care because I was almost fifty and that's when you stop caring so much about what other people think, and anyway it didn't matter how I sang, but why.

Something burst into flame inside when I sang though. I felt that I was communicating something of myself that I couldn't speak in mere words. Something deep. Something spiritual.

Listening to music was always something that I loved too. From early in my teens, I collected music whenever and wherever I could. I loved rare albums and would scour music stores in the city for limited release records. I soon had an extensive collection of rarities, which disappeared once I left home and dad cleaned out my room. Shame.

Music was another thing which kept my head above water during my struggle with PTSD. Not so much singing and playing but certainly listening. Most days I could not face singing and playing. It was too hard, too raw. It threatened to show too much of the pain that was inside and I just wasn't ready to do that. I was still in "fight, flight or freeze mode" and consequently was still cocooned from all that might come to threaten any form of barrier that I had put up.

But listening. Listening was different. Listening at that stage was cathartic. It was messy and sad and brought me to tears often but I saw that this was necessary. It was salve to the wound; a salve that at that point in time couldn't and wouldn't bring total healing but served to numb the pain. Listening to the songs of others showed me, if nothing else, that pain was universal; that there were others out there who understood, had been there and had maybe come out the other side.

One band that I devoured during this time was Jars of Clay. An indie band that I had always respected, their lyrics came to the fore and were salve to my wound on the most painful of days. They were a band who spoke of faith and art – two areas which resonated in me. They were honest. Like me, they took hold of pain and questioning, picked it up, turned it over and examined it, no matter how painful. They asked the hard questions and were not afraid to find there weren't answers straight away, or that if there were, they were not the expected, trite, comfortable ones.

I would always listen to music while running. Always. It took me to a place, away from where I was, even if only for a short time. I always came back but for that brief period, I was transported. Music and running were my meditation – and a medication that was proving far more effective than the mega doses of drugs that I had been prescribed.

And so, in the dead of winter 2012, in the fog of PTSD and depression, I took to running the beach. Maybe it was a metaphor of the state of my mind. Bitterly cold, bleak, windswept, I was drawn to it. I couldn't keep away. The beach at Goolwa sweeps around to the west towards Middleton, Port Elliot and eventually Victor Harbor. There were quite a few people in that direction and there were many days when I ran to Middleton and back (12kms) or, if I was feeling really good, Port Elliot and back (16 kms). But if I headed towards the south-east…

The south-east…

In that direction, hundreds of kilometres of beach and sandhills stretched out with hardly a person save for fisher people who travelled in their four wheel drives along the ten kilometre stretch from the Goolwa Beach car park to the Murray Mouth. Beyond the Murray Mouth lay the true Coorong – a windswept series of sandhills and lagoons, separated from the sea by a thin stretch of sandhills. A desolate, rugged beauty. That place was way beyond my reach but I yearned for it.

It was this direction that drew me on my runs. There was something there on my beach. I was certain as I ran it, kilometre after kilometre, day after day, hunting for something, anything that would answer the questions in my head that were demanding reconciliation. The silence and desolation of the beach mirrored that which was present in my heart and mind. I found a strange, cathartic comfort in the pain.

And as I ran the beach, I listened to my music. One song, a Jars of Clay song, above all shouted to the elements about the struggle I was having.

Silence[1]

Take
Take till there's nothing
Nothing to turn to
Nothing when you get through
Won't you break
Scattered pieces of all I've been
Bowing to all I've been
Running to
Where are you?
Where are you?

Did
Did you leave me unbreakable?
You leave me frozen?
I've never felt so cold
I thought you were silent
And I thought you left me
For the wreckage and the waste

---

[1] Copyright © 2002 Pogostick Music (BMI) Pogostick Music (BMI) Pogostick Music (BMI) Bridge Building Music (BMI) Pogostick Music (BMI) (adm. at CapitolCMGPublishing.com) All rights reserved. Used by permission.

Silence

On an empty beach of faith
Was it true?

Cuz I...I got a question
I got a question
Where are you?

Scream
Deeper I wanna scream
I want you to hear me
I want you to find me
Cuz I...I want to believe
But all I pray is wrong
And all I claim is gone

And I...I got a question
I got a question
Where are you?
Yeah....yeah
And where...I...I got a question
I got a question
Where are you?
Where are you?
Where are you?
Where are you?

My beach became the metaphor of my struggle.

I *did* feel so alone.

I *had* never felt so cold.

And in reply to all of the questions I had, all I heard was the silence of a deserted, remote South Australian beach. The occasional gull, the howl of a southerly gale straight off the Antarctic, that I pressed into day after day, and the incessant crash of the waves on my shore. A beautiful silence now that I reflect on it but one which I regarded with despair at the seeming wreckage and waste of my life and the questions about how I would possibly ever get it all back together again. When I set this silence up against the silence I luxuriated in on the first night of our arrival on the South Coast, the two seemed worlds apart. I see now that perhaps they were closer than it seemed at the time, and possibly not as black and white.

"Where are You in all of this? I can't see You." My faith told me that I was not alone but my head was experiencing something much, much different.

And so I ran my empty beach of faith, day after day, week after week, month after month, from the first year into the next, listening, searching for a reply among the wreckage. But there was nothing. Just silence.

In late 2013, I was browsing the Internet and just happened to come across the Jars of Clay website. I had been there before many times but for some reason this time, I looked at their touring schedule.

It was one of "those" moments when I was acting without thought. It was that night with Robert, when I called him without being aware. It was that day with Azim, when a small voice whispered to me, "Follow him." A gentle whisper out of the silence.

On a whim, before I really knew what I was doing, I emailed them, asking if they were ever going to come to Australia. To my surprise, a few days later I had a reply from Charlie, a member of the band. He said that they

Silence

were in fact coming to Australia, to Queensland, in April, Easter, the following year.

I emailed back and told them about our son Josh, who has a developmental disorder and how music had never appealed to him until I introduced him to their music. He had become a huge fan, and listening to their music had opened him up to the world in a way that I just didn't understand. Charlie emailed me back saying how cool that was and how they would love to meet him one day.

That started something in me.

I mulled over it for a long time but eventually talked to my boys and we decided to do the three day drive to Queensland to see Jars of Clay in concert. The concert was part of a festival and looking at the schedule, I could see that they would only be performing for just under an hour. Three days of driving for less than an hour? Crazy, I know, but there was something driving me. I knew I had to be there. There were ten thousand others going but I needed to be there.

And so we booked and planned our trip.

We arrived at our destination Thursday night, set ourselves up in our accommodation for the week and got some sleep; pretty exhausted after the drive. We planned to register at the festival the next day and then my first mission was to get Josh to meet the band.

Next morning we were up and away early. We registered, entered the park venue and then I set about finding someone "in charge." There were some volunteers there who were responsible for caring for the artists appearing. I took my time observing them and then went up to one of them – a lady (and I am so sorry, I can't remember your name. Know though, that you played such a role in my return to life. Pivotal).

I introduced myself, told her our story and showed her the email from Charlie that I had saved on my iPad. When I shared about Josh, her eyes lit up and she exclaimed, "Say no more! I used to be a special ed teacher. Leave it with me." She took our details and said she'd get back to us.

Incredible, out of all of the volunteers I could have chosen, I chose one who used to work in the same profession as me, and who was on a similar wavelength. Just incredible.

We heard back from her a little later in the day. She had organised for us to meet Jars of Clay before their concert that night. We were to go to the front of the venue, side stage, and introduce ourselves to someone and then be led back to meet them. Josh was so wired. He kept asking me how long it would be from several hours out. He was extremely nervous and despite the heat of Queensland, was wearing his Jars of Clay hoodie, beanie and scarf. He was ready.

Seven o'clock arrived. The time we were to meet them. We followed the instructions and went side stage. There were consultations between "crowd management", glances back our way, and then Josh and I were ushered backstage. Tim at the time was in the mosh-pit and I couldn't get his attention.

We arrived backstage and there were Josh's heroes, in the flesh. They were real – which for him, I think, was a bit of a shock. We said "hi", shook hands and posed for photos. It was so wonderful for Josh and I could see in his eyes that it had just made his life…

We then took up our positions front of stage for the concert. It was everything Josh had imagined and more. His eyes were shining. He loved every moment of it.

After the concert, we rushed out to meet the guys as they went to an autograph signing session. We managed to get Tim in a photo with some of the boys and we briefly chatted. I showed some of my iPad photos of Josh's artwork. It was all quite surreal for him.

Silence

That night, after we arrived back at our unit, I put together a brief thank you email. In it, I shared how much it had meant to Josh. Then, again, on a whim, I shared about part of my PTSD journey – very briefly about the initial incident, the resultant descent into PTSD but more so about running my empty beach of faith, listening to their song, "Silence."

The next day, again, there was a reply from Charlie, this one empathising with me about my journey and thanking me for sharing.

After that, it was a full weekend of music and interviews and we caught up with the boys a few more times. Each time they were so gracious with their time. Really genuine men. We didn't want to be seen to be stalkers but I'm sure that deep down, they may have been beginning to worry. I just wanted Josh in particular, to have the best weekend. Tim and I were both happy anyway. There was music!

We caught up with them after a TV interview session they had, which the public were invited to sit in on. After the interview, I decided to be brave. We had driven so far for so long, I felt that it was time to throw caution to the wind and just be brave. People could always say, "No."

You see, the band were to be playing a concert for VIP ticket holders later that day – Easter Sunday. We didn't have a VIP ticket. So I asked Dan and Charlie if there was any way we could get in. Dan spoke to his minder and asked him if there was any way that the organisers would let us in. They arranged it so we could. Josh was pumped. Absolutely pumped.

So, the afternoon of Easter Sunday arrived. We lined up at the front of the queue, ticketless, wearing the wrong colour wristband. I felt like we stuck out like a sore thumb, and that there were whispered comments about us amongst those with the correct colour wristband. Paranoid, I know. An organiser eventually came out, apologising for the delay. They were making sure that the sound was right. I introduced myself after she eyed my incorrect colour wristband with suspicion and asked if she could confirm my story with the band. She didn't seem too keen and I began to become rather doubtful about whether we would make it in.

Silence: A Spiritual Journey Through PTSD

She disappeared for about twenty minutes but then reappeared and confirmed the story, "Are you lucky. I wasn't going to let you in." Huge sigh of relief.

We secured front row seats for the concert. As it turned out, the band were not performing their latest album as advertised because they had sung most of the tracks at the first concert. Instead, they performed a selection from across their twenty year career. Many of my favourites were included, and I began to think that they were singing just for me.

And then…

Towards the end of the concert, Dan introduced the next song simply, saying, "This song is dedicated to some new friends that we have made this weekend. This is for Andrew and his family." Twenty one words that I will never, ever forget.

His words did not quite register for a while but then began the opening bars of the song that I had pounded the beach to, kilometre after kilometre, month after month, searching desperately for answers… and healing.

Take
Take till there's nothing
Nothing to turn to
Nothing when you get through
Won't you break
Scattered pieces of all I've been
Bowing to all I've been
Running to
Where are you?
Where are you?

Silence

As the song unfolded, tears began to pool in my eyes. Salty tears born on a beach of faith. For a time, I wiped them away but shortly I could not wipe them away. They started streaming down my face. I was so conscious of my boys next to me, watching. The other people around didn't matter so much. I would never see them again. In the end, I decided not to contain the tears any more. I had lived the past two years trying to contain them, cocooning myself from the pain and I was tired of it. So, so tired. I let go.

I thought You left me
For the wreckage and the waste
On an empty beach of faith
Was it true?

Soon, the tears could not be controlled and I was a blubbering mess. I desperately wanted to lie prostrated on the ground and wail but I knew that would be a bit off-putting for the other concert goers. So I sat, head in hands, weeping, unashamed, unfettered, soaking in a song which had been so special to me, sung… for me.

Scream
Deeper I wanna scream
I want you to hear me
I want you to find me
Cuz I…I want to believe
But all I pray is wrong
And all I claim is gone

As the tears fell, something happened that I didn't notice until several weeks later. It was as if all of the pent up pain, all of the darkness of the previous two years, were simply washed away in my tears. I was transported to my beach: the wind, the waves, the sand, the endless pounding and searching, the silence… and I finally found something. I don't know what that something was. Mystery. Intangible, but something so, so precious… and healing. Even now, as I write this, a considerable amount of time down the track, it still affects me emotionally.

I went up to Charlie and Dan afterwards and thanked them so much. I couldn't say anything really and may have used a lot of sign language. I don't know. I was so overcome. Apart from my wife agreeing to marry me, I think it was simply the nicest thing that anyone has ever done for me.

Blind but now I see

I didn't realise it immediately but in the weeks and months that followed this extraordinary moment, I came to believe that I had been healed from the emotional and mental torment of PTSD. I don't make this statement lightly. Not only that, I noticed too that the dark cloud that had been my ever-present but never-welcome companion since the age of about 15, was no longer there. I had come to the point some time during my journey through PTSD where I understood that I had been living with depression for more than thirty years.

As I mentioned earlier, depression became my unwelcome companion when I was halfway through high school. I know what triggered this condition but I'm not going to go into details here because I simply don't feel comfortable sharing it. Suffice to say, the triggering events lasted about a year and to say that they had a profound effect on these formative years is a massive understatement. The last couple of years of high school were a blur and I remember having trouble getting into any sort of study routine and consequently bombing out in a couple of subjects in Year 12. Of course, the fact that my school counsellor recommended three maths and science subjects, and just two of the humanities didn't help. However, I was in such a daze because of what was happening in my life, that I just went along with the recommendation.

But after the concert moment which I have described in the previous chapter, depression too was no longer there. Each morning as I woke, something extraordinary happened which hadn't occurred for thirty or so years. The sun came out. The dark cloud which had been the first thing I was aware of from the moment I woke up for many of my mornings from my mid teens to my mid 40s did not reform. And now, as I edit this little paragraph eight years later, the dark cloud has not reformed.

The black cloud of depression has gradually been replaced by a cloud of a different kind. A cloud of unknowing. A cloud which can most of the time graciously accept that I cannot know the answer to all things; that I cannot say easily or with any certainty what is "good" or "bad" for me. There are treasures to be found and often they are only found as we search in darkness. Nothing is wasted. I believe this to be true. Nothing. Not the good, nor the bad. Not the peaceful or the chaotic. Not riches or poverty. Not noise or silence. God is making all things new.

As I said, I don't say all of this lightly. I've never been one for fanfare or making myself the centre of attention. I'd much rather be backstage than centre-stage. The thought of acting terrifies me. The thought of directing in the background thrills. But I can't deny that since that moment, I don't feel the same way.

The lyrics of the much loved song, *Amazing Grace* state, "I once was lost but now I'm found, was blind but now I see." Oh, how I can relate to this. You see, for decades, I thought everyone had a dark cloud following them. I didn't realise until the sun came out, and burned every drop of dark vapour away, that this wasn't the case. I kept waiting for the storm cloud to regather over my head, but now seven years later it still hasn't returned. That's not to say that I don't have my down days, or experience sadness. But it's a "good" sadness, a sadness that shows to me that I care about someone or something; it's not the unrelenting blackness that is depression. I know how I was then and how I am now. I was blind but now I see.

I still shake my head in wonder every single day, even after all this time.

As I have described elsewhere here, the "Wounded Healer" concept has always resonated deeply in me. Being honest in my journey, especially during the years of shadow and darkness, has been paramount to me. I am one who has believed from a fairly young age that it is important to take pain, pick it up, turn it over and examine it, in order to understand it, so that in time I might be life and breath for someone else who may be struggling with something similar. Life is a song not scored for breathing. It is a quest with a fellowship in a life and death struggle. I sometimes need others to breathe for me and in time, I pray to be breath for those who gasp for oxygen.

Without the scars that pain leaves behind we lack power to see the pain in others. Without our cracks, seams of gold cannot be created. It is indeed our melancholy that makes our voices reverberate in the troubled hearts of others. Being broken on the wheels of living is indeed the most powerfully persuasive way of leading others to healing.

I will never ever forget that moment on Easter Sunday 2014 (tears here right now) at a music festival in Queensland, when a keyboard started playing a simple descending three note melody, and the words of a song that was so dear to me came crashing from the stage, like the waves of the Southern Ocean on my beloved beach of faith. At that moment, my world died, went down into a watery grave of flooding tears and rose again, all shiny and new.

Lessons from the Road #3

And sometimes when you're running
You remember all those things:
About just getting to the next pole, or the next minute
Or the next step
And about how the wind will be your friend
On the homeward run

You remember all those things
And you start out with confidence
But sometimes even before you're halfway
It just gets too hard
And you don't care about the goals you've set
For the day
Or the week
Or the month
Because you just have no energy left for the run

And you have to admit defeat this time
And stop
And take a breath
And regather your thoughts
And turn for home
And not worry that
You haven't made it through this time
And remember that this is just a small step
In what will hopefully be a much longer journey
That this day will not define your life

Victorious Limp

I love the movie *Les Miserables* with Geoffrey Rush as Javert and Liam Neeson as Valjean. There is a scene at the end of the movie, where Javert reconciles – logically to his legalistic mind – allowing Valjean to go free, by drowning himself in the river. After he explains his logic to a confused Valjean, he releases Valjean from the handcuffs, clips them onto his own hands, says to Valjean, "You're free" and falls backwards into the murky waters.

After Javert vanishes into the murky waters of the Seine, Valjean stands for a time, just watching in disbelief, not completely comprehending what has just occurred. But then he turns from the river and starts walking along the street. Slowly at first, with a noticeable limp but then with an increasing pace. He looks into the sky, his eyes slowly beginning to convey the understanding that somehow, against all human logic, he has been released from decades of imprisonment. Not a literal one but the imprisonment of knowing that at any moment, Javert could have found him and sent him back to prison. It is a look of gratitude and disbelief and freedom and thankfulness. Tears begin to pour down his face, as he raises his head skyward. It is finished.

And that is how I felt after that concert moment. In the weeks and months that followed, I began to become aware of feelings of gratitude and disbelief and freedom and thankfulness. But most of all, a lightness which is impossible to describe to anyone who has not lived under the impossible weight of depression, or PTSD, or both, or any other form of mental illness. The dark cloud was no longer there. The weight of the world that had burdened me for most of my life fell away. I now work as a counsellor for people living with disability, either their own, or someone in their family. One metaphor that I often use is to think of a goldfish in its fishbowl. It just swims around in its bowl, day after day, no matter the state of the water. It doesn't notice the water's quality or the effect that this environment is having on its health. It simply swims. And that is how it had been for me. Depression had been clouding the water of my fishbowl for decades but I wasn't aware of it. I just kept swimming, albeit against the tide, thinking this was normal.

But then, the water cleared.

As I reflected in the months and years after this moment, my thoughts were mainly neurological, due to the psychological study that I took up. During the original incident with Azim, a neural pathway was burned so deeply in my brain that it was triggered easily by any little thing associated with the incident. It needed something to short circuit it… enter stage left, Jars of Clay and Easterfest events. Not discounting Spirit work at all, but the new event short circuited the original one. It was a Spirit filled event of such magnitude that it burnt a new neural pathway, wiping away completely the memories of horror of what happened, replacing them with much more pleasant ones. That became the new neural pathway. Stunning stuff!

I'm not saying that it will happen in the same way for everyone. PTSD, depression and other mental illnesses debilitate and decimate countless lives the world over every day and there are no easy answers. The neural pathways are deeply grooved and need new pathways to bypass the old. For me, I see that the Jars of Clay concert event was the key because it short circuited the neural pathway I was wandering helplessly down every day for two years. Jesus said that He was making all things new. As I briefly shared my story with Charlie via email after my son's dream date, I see that I was offering up my pain, being open and sharing my story with another. That pain was taken up and transformed when "my" song was sung on that Easter Sunday.

And for all who suffer a similar debilitation, I firmly believe the answer is that a new neural pathway, a more powerful one, needs to be forged in some way. Just as travellers into Narnia didn't always arrive by way of a wardrobe door, so it is on the pathway to healing from mental illness. It's not going to happen the same way for everyone.

We are truly fearfully and wonderfully made creatures. I'm so glad there is still a lot of room allowed, in my life at least, for Mystery and Wonder. My prayer for all of 2013 and into 2014 for other people, had been simply, "God, do something unexpected." I never ever thought it would happen for me.

Now, almost inexplicably, I am so thankful for all that happened that day in 2012 with Azim and even now, ten years later, I shake my head in wonder and gratitude at all that happened and how completely my walk changed. But as I walked from that day, I, like Valjean, noticed a limp in my gait. It didn't come for a number of years later, but in time I realised that though the mental symptoms of PTSD and depression were gone, the physical toll on my body remained and frustrated me (and continues to) almost every day since. For the consequence of running on adrenaline for two years is not comfortable and it left my physical body in a bit of a mess. And that mess is still a daily struggle, some eight years after the wonderful events of 2014. But that's a story for another time.

And so I too walk with a limp. It is a limp of one who has been wounded. But nothing is wasted and as I came to see, it's hard to judge what is good and what is bad, I began to apply these redemption ideas to the physical effects I continued to experience. I hoped the limp would reveal to others that I had been through something and, to those brave enough, they might just ask. And, as I shared my story with them, hopefully we would find further healing and comfort and encouragement in the sharing of each other's stories.

Yes, I limp. It probably will never go away completely because when we are damaged, the scars, the reminders never entirely dissipate, as on days when the weather conditions are a certain way, and a war veteran feels the pain in his or her leg or arm and is reminded again of the trauma and horror of battle.

Yes, I limp but it is a victorious one. It is a limp that also conveys gratitude and disbelief and freedom and gratitude, and gratitude and gratitude.

As we walk our silent beaches of faith, I wonder if that's the best anyone can do.

Epilogue: For Maggie

Oh Maggie. Thank you for choosing me. I will miss you so much. Heartbroken.

Faithful, faithful friend. We hear this about dogs all the time. Faithful, loyal. But Maggie …

Maggie and I had such a bond. I always referred to her jokingly, as "my second best friend." But the truth is, there was Sally (and the kids of course), then there was Maggie, and after that, daylight. Moving down south was wonderful in so many ways for us and I would never ever think of moving back to the city. But one way in which it wasn't so great for me was in terms of friendships.

I'm not the type who has a lot of friends. I keep my circle close. I have written somewhere else in these pages about fellowship. About going on a great quest with my friends. I had a few people in Adelaide of which I would say that was true. But the effect of moving down south was I was suddenly without my tribe, save for my family, and I wasn't about to develop new friendships quickly.

And so, when that day with Azim happened, and I crashed, I had no one apart from Sally and the kids (and the kids weren't old enough yet to be able to carry me) humanly speaking, to lean on. No one else came and sat alongside me in the pain.

Apart from Maggie. This beautiful, gentle, stubborn, thoroughly disobedient soul who lay with me faithfully, day after day, week after week, month after month, from one year into the next. No judgement, no expectations, no demands, no trite statements. Just a patient, adoring soul who sat with me in my darkness.

And so, when she died three days after my birthday in 2019, five years after PTSD had been dealt with, her passing hit me like a B-Double. The day she passed and for several weeks afterwards, I was inconsolable. Utterly devastated.

And that was okay.

As I reflected on it, I could see that in terms of grief, this was my first real experience with it. Apart from grandparents, no one in my immediate family had died. Maggie was the first.

The day after she died, I spent some time building a memorial to her in a quiet, secluded spot on our two and half acres. As the winter wind howled around me, I hauled rocks in my arms, tears streaming down my face, and at times crying out aloud, from one side of the block to the other. It was messy and wet and loud and ugly. But it was also a beautiful time. In the hauling of rocks, I felt that I was honouring her passing, showing her that she was important, and that she wouldn't be forgotten by me. And not forgotten by anyone who visited our house and happened to take a stroll outside. They would stop and look and see that Maggie had lived here and she had been a special one.

It gave me a place to go in the days, weeks and months that followed when it all got too hard. Because the truth is that in the days and weeks and months that followed, tears hit me from out of the blue. And when it happened, I let them fall, unashamed of who saw them. And if people asked me if I was okay, I would gently explain to them what had happened. And some, many, would nod in understanding and share their stories of when it had happened to them. This created a bond, a fellowship.

I've been thinking a lot about beauty lately. I've been thinking a lot about where True Beauty lies. Where it can be found and why our eyes and our hearts are dazzled by it when we recognise it. I wonder if True Beauty emerges from ugliness, from chaos. In the Beginning, there was chaos. Everything was formless, if there even was an everything. But from the chaos, the Spirit breathed a Word and Beauty emerged...

A Man stumbles wounded, bleeding, through an angry, seething, ugly crowd. Hateful words are spat at Him as He passes, eyes fixed firmly on the hill up ahead, even though He can't see it because of all the people.

Epilogue: For Maggie

But He knows that it lies ahead. His eyes have been resolutely fixed on it for years. And He staggers through the ugliness, and He is nailed to ugliness, and He dies by the hand of ugliness and for ugliness....

And creation stands silent. Expectant. Holding its groan for an extended moment...

And from behind an insignificant, ugly stone, one of thousands of billions of stones in the universe, True Beauty emerges.

And everything is changed...

And Maggie died and I buried her under ugly stones. She didn't rise again in physical form. But she did rise in my heart. She rises in it each and every day still and the tears still fill my eyes when I think of her, even today two years after her death.

And she is truly beautiful...

www.ingramcontent.com/pod-product-compliance
Lightning Source LLC
Chambersburg PA
CBHW020323010526
44107CB00054B/1951